© Crown copyright 2007. Published with the permission of the DfES on behalf of the Controller of Her Majesty's Stationery Office.

Applications for reproduction should be made in writing to the Copyright Unit, Her Majesty's Stationery Office, St Clements House, 2-16 Colegate, Norwich NR3 1BQ

ISBN 978 0 11 271193 3

Published by TSO (The Stationery Office) and available from:

Online
www.tsoshop.co.uk

Mail, Telephone, Fax & E-mail
TSO, PO Box 29, Norwich, NR3 1GN
Telephone orders/General enquiries: 0870 600 5522
Fax orders: 0870 600 5533
E-mail: customer.services@tso.co.uk
Textphone 0870 240 3701

TSO Shops
123 Kingsway, London, WC2B 6PQ
020 7242 6393 Fax 020 7242 6394
16 Arthur Street, Belfast BT1 4GD
028 9023 8451 Fax 028 9023 5401
71 Lothian Road, Edinburgh EH3 9AZ
0870 606 5566 Fax 0870 606 5588

TSO Accredited Agents
(see Yellow Pages)

TSO@Blackwell and other Accredited Agents

N5523591 C100 02/07

Contents

In-year fair access protocols

Admission of children of UK Service personnel and other Crown servants (including Diplomats) outside the normal admission round

Timing of admissions

Admission Authorities

Local Authorities

Admission Forums

Objections by Parents

The Schools Adjudicator

APPENDICES

Sex Discrimination Act 1975

Race Relations Act 1976 and 2000

Human Rights Act 1998

Disability Discrimination Acts 1995 and 2005

Equality Act 2006

Admission Appeals

Membership

Tenure

Procedure for meetings and appointment of officers

Promulgating advice and making objections

Agreeing schemes for admission to secondary schools

Schemes imposed by the Secretary of State

Main obligations imposed by regulations

Applications to schools with a different age transfer

Foreword by the Secretary of State

Parents want their children to be able to attend a good school where they will be happy and secure and able to learn and thrive. As it's one of the most important decisions a parent will make, it is no surprise that school admissions arouse strong feelings.

The Government is committed to supporting parents not least by ensuring that every school is a good school and that the system as a whole offers as much choice and diversity as possible. While we recognise that in some cases only one school is within a reasonable travelling distance, in England 77% of households have at least two secondary schools within 2 miles and 95% have two or more primary schools within 2 miles.

In order to deliver a diverse and excellent system, schools can become autonomous self governing schools with governing bodies able to determine their own admission arrangements in response to the needs of their communities. This Code and the related legislation will ensure that admission authorities – whether local authorities or schools – operate in a fair way that promotes social equity and community cohesion.

This Code has a stronger statutory basis than its predecessors. All admission authorities are required to *act in accordance* with its mandatory provisions (whereas they had only to have regard to earlier versions). The Education and Inspections Act 2006 ends the practice of schools interviewing children and their families for school places. The Code rules out completely a number of unacceptable oversubscription criteria such as taking account of a parent's occupation, financial or marital status and ends the 'first preference first' criterion that made the system unnecessarily complex for parents. Parents also have important new rights to object to the Office of the Schools Adjudicator if they believe that any aspect of a school's admission arrangements fail to comply with the law or mandatory requirements imposed by the Code.

Local authorities – and other schools – also continue to have critical roles to play. Local authorities in particular, as the commissioner of services and champion of parents, are expected to be vigilant in assessing the admission arrangements of schools in its area and objecting to unfair practices.

We are also widening membership of Admission Forums and adding to their powers. All schools will in future automatically be members of their local forum and the forum will have the power to produce an annual report on how well the admission arrangements of all schools are serving the interests of all pupils. These reports will provide important contributions to the biennial reports of the Schools Commissioner on fair access.

Most parents are able to find the information they need to decide which schools to apply for their children. But for some, the system can be confusing and they may need help to decide which schools they would like to apply for. This is why the Government has provided funding for local authorities to provide a Choice Advice service specifically to target advice and assistance at those families who need the most help in choosing a secondary school for their child that best meets their needs.

The law and this Code also make special arrangements for the most vulnerable children. Schools will continue to be required to admit children with statements of special educational need where the school concerned is named on the statement. Children who are in public care (looked after children) must now be given top priority in the oversubscription criteria for all schools. And because these children often have to move school during the school year, the law gives their corporate parent the crucial right to direct any school to give them a place, even where the school is full.

Over the past few years, most local authorities have worked with their schools to establish protocols to ensure that all schools take a fair share of children who are hard to place. The Code now puts these protocols - which we have renamed in-year fair access protocols - on a mandatory footing: all local authorities will be required to produce one and all schools will be required to participate in them.

I know that the vast majority of schools are committed to equity and to fair access. I am certain that this Code is a great step towards fair access for all pupils and fair arrangements in all schools.

ALAN JOHNSON

Introduction

The Statutory Basis for the School Admissions Code

1. The School Admissions Code (the Code) comes into force on 28 February 2007, and applies to admissions to all maintained schools[1] and Academies.

2. Admission authorities **must** ensure that their determined admission arrangements for 2008 comply with the mandatory provisions of this Code. The School Admissions (Alteration and Variation of, and Objections to, Arrangements)(England)(Amendment) Regulations 2007 permit admission authorities to amend their determined admission arrangements without reference to the Schools Adjudicator to ensure that they comply with the law and the mandatory provisions of this Code.

3. This Code is made under section 84 of the School Standards and Framework Act 1998 as amended by section 40 of the Education and Inspections Act 2006. Section 84(2) provides that the Code may impose requirements and may include guidelines setting out aims, objectives and other matters in relation to the discharge of functions by the bodies listed at paragraph 10 below. Section 84(3) requires these bodies to act in accordance with the provisions of the Code. References to 'the Code' or 'this Code' include the foreword, this introduction, the chapters, appendices and glossary. This Code has been made following a consultation under section 85(2) of the School Standards and Framework Act 1998, as provided by section 40(9) of the Education and Inspections Act 2006, and having been laid before each House for 40 days as provided by section 85(3) of the 1998 Act. The Secretary of State has therefore issued it in the form of the draft under section 85(5) of the 1998 Act. This Code and related information are available at www.dfes.gov.uk/sacode.

---

[1] This includes grammar schools, Trust schools, boarding schools, and for entry into school sixth forms.

4.   The Code imposes mandatory requirements and refers to statutory requirements (i.e. those imposed by primary or secondary legislation) with which those bodies listed at paragraph 10 below **must** comply. References to the relevant statutory provisions are provided in the text and footnotes. Full citations of the regulations referred to in the footnotes of this Code and details of amending instruments can be found at www.dfes.gov.uk/sacode, and references to Acts are abbreviated as follows:

a)   Education Act 1996 – EA 1996

b)   School Standards and Framework Act 1998 – SSFA 1998

c)   Education Act 2002 – EA 2002

d)   Education Act 2005 – EA 2005

e)   Education and Inspections Act 2006 – EIA 2006

5.   Where mandatory requirements are imposed by this Code (or by statutory provisions) it is stated that relevant bodies **'must'** comply with the particular requirement or provision. Where this Code prohibits practices or criteria it is stated that relevant body or bodies **'must not'** use the practices or criteria. Where the requirement is imposed by primary or secondary legislation this is indicated.

6.   The Code also includes guidelines which the relevant bodies should follow unless they can demonstrate, if challenged, that they are justified in not doing so. Where guidelines refer to good practice the Code will state that the relevant bodies **'should'** follow the particular guidelines and where the guidelines refer to practices or criteria normally regarded as poor practice, but where there may be exceptional circumstances when they may be justified, the Code will state that the practices or criteria **'should not'** be used.

7.   In this Code the following terms have the following meanings:

a)   'Admission arrangements' means the overall procedure, practices and criteria to be used in deciding on the allocation of school places.

b)   'Admission practice' refers to any device or means used to determine whether a school place is to be offered (e.g. supplementary application or information forms).

c)   'Oversubscription criteria' refers to the criteria used to decide on the allocation of places when a school has more applications than places available.

8. Failure by an authority or body included in paragraph 10 below to comply with the mandatory requirements in this Code is a breach of that authority's or body's statutory duty to act in accordance with the provisions of this Code. Failure to comply with the mandatory provisions in the Code may result in an objection being made to the Schools Adjudicator or a complaint to the Secretary of State (see paragraph 13).

9. Failure to follow the guidelines in this Code may lead to a challenge and admission authorities will have to be able to demonstrate that they were justified in departing from those guidelines. If they cannot do so an objection may be upheld by the Schools Adjudicator.

10. This Code applies to the following bodies:

   a) **Admission authorities:** local authorities are the admission authorities for community and voluntary controlled schools, unless the function has been delegated to the governing body[2]. For foundation schools (including Trust schools[3]), voluntary-aided schools and Academies[4], governing bodies are the admission authority.

   b) **Governing bodies (when not admission authorities)**

   c) **Local authorities (when not acting as admission authorities)**

   d) **Admission Forums**

   e) **Schools Adjudicators**

   f) **Admission appeal panels**

11. Admission authorities **must** ensure that any member of staff employed at the school has no individual role in the admission process (see paragraph 1.45). This does not affect the individual's role as a member of the governing body.

---

[2] Section 88(1) of the SSFA 1998.
[3] All foundation schools with foundations are popularly known as 'Trust schools'.
[4] Academies are independent, mixed ability schools, established with sponsors under section 482 of the EA 1996 (as substituted by section 65 of the EA 2002). The funding agreement between an Academy company and the Secretary of State requires the Academy's admissions policy and arrangements to be consistent with admissions law and the School Admissions Code.

Monitoring compliance with the Code

12. Admission Forums[5] will monitor compliance with this Code, and the overall impact of the admission arrangements in an area on fair access. They have powers under section 85A(1A) of the School Standards and Framework Act 1998 (as inserted by section 41(3) of the Education and Inspections Act 2006) to produce an annual report on admission arrangements in their area covering information that may include the number of preferences met and the social and ethnic mix of schools compared with that of the communities they serve or in which they are located. These reports may be used by local authorities in discharging their functions and by the Schools Commissioner in advising the Secretary of State. More detailed information on Admission Forums and their role in monitoring compliance with this Code can be found in Chapter 4 and Appendix 2.

Enforcing the Code

13. Decisions on objections to admission arrangements are made by the Schools Adjudicator. Local authorities, other local schools and Admission Forums have important powers under section 90 of the School Standards and Framework Act 1998 to refer admission arrangements to the Adjudicator where the admission authority concerned fails to comply with the mandatory provisions of this Code, or where they do not follow its guidelines. Local authorities are required by this Code (paragraph 4.6) to refer the admission arrangements of any school to the Adjudicator if it appears to them that they do not comply with the law or the mandatory requirements of this Code.

14. Parents[6] may also object to the Adjudicator if admission arrangements contain practices or criteria that they consider do not comply with the law or the mandatory provisions of this Code. Faith groups may object to the admission arrangements of schools of their faith. Effective enforcement of this Code by the Adjudicator relies on the proper exercise of these powers.

---

[5] Admission Forums derive their powers from sections 85A and 85B of the SSFA 1998 as inserted by the EA 2002 and amended by the EIA 2006, and from The Education (Admission Forums) (England) Regulations 2002 (SI 2002 /2900) as amended by SI 2007/192.

[6] Section 576 of the EA 1996 provides that in relation to a young person or child, the term 'parent' includes any person who is not a parent of his but who has parental responsibility (as defined by the Children Act 1989) or who has care of him.

15. The Adjudicator's determination of objections is final and the parties affected are required to implement that determination. If they do not, the Secretary of State may direct them to do so under section 497 (or section 496) of the Education Act 1996. More detailed information on the role of the Schools Adjudicator in enforcing this Code can be found in Chapter 4.

Chapter 1

The Law: Equity and Fair Access in School Admission Arrangements

This chapter provides guidelines on the law and achieving fair access in school admission arrangements:

- Duties to increase opportunities for parental choice, respond to parental representations, and improve community cohesion (1.8)

- Admissions: key statutory provisions (1.14)

- Co-ordinated admission schemes (1.16)

- Considering applications for school places (1.28)

- Children from overseas (1.52)

- Ensuring equity and fair access (1.64)

- Practices and policies that may undermine fair admission arrangements (1.70)

- Prohibition of supplementary information forms (1.71)

- School uniforms (1.80)

- School transport (1.87)

- Being proactive about extending opportunity and fair access for all (1.90)

1.1 Educational achievement is critical to the life chances of all our children and is at the heart of the Government's Every Child Matters strategy[7]. While heavily influenced by factors beyond the school, achievement at school also has a direct influence on other aspects of children's well-being, for example childhood and adult health, crime, anti-social behaviour and economic competitiveness. Because of this, it is important that all children from all backgrounds, races and religions, have the same opportunities to go to good quality schools.

1.2 Teaching, learning and standards in schools are improving. But too many children fall short of the standards they could – and need to – achieve. Attainment gaps between children of different social backgrounds are not closing fast enough and too many of the children facing the greatest disadvantages are also attending the poorest performing schools. Local authorities have new powers, under sections 63 to 66 of the Education and Inspections Act 2006, to tackle under-performing schools promptly and to ensure that the very worst schools, which are judged by Ofsted as requiring special measures, are turned round more swiftly and decisively. It is also necessary to improve the chances of more disadvantaged children getting into good schools.

1.3 This new School Admissions Code underpins the Government's aim to create a schools system shaped by parents which delivers excellence and equity, developing the talents and potential of every child, regardless of their background; **a system where all parents feel they have the same opportunities to apply for the schools they want for their child.**

1.4 This chapter briefly sets out the key statutory provisions that underpin school admissions; it also imposes mandatory requirements and provides guidelines on ensuring fair admission arrangements that promote equity. In determining their admission arrangements, admission authorities should read the provisions and guidelines in this chapter in conjunction with the guidelines and requirements set out in Chapters 2 and 3 and relevant Appendices 1 to 4.

1.5 A fair system needs to provide parents with access to good information about admissions in order to support those parents who find it hardest to understand the system.

---

[7] www.everychildmatters.gov.uk

1.6 Local authorities are required to provide advice and assistance to all parents of children of all ages in their area when they are expressing a preference of school for their child (section 86(1A) of the School Standards and Framework Act 1998, as inserted by section 42 of the Education and Inspections Act 2006). In discharging this duty in the case of transition from primary to secondary school, local authorities **should** establish a Choice Advice service. Choice Advice targets practical support and advice at those parents who are most likely to need extra help in navigating the admissions system. Choice Advice can be delivered flexibly using a range of models to meet local circumstances but local authorities **must** provide an independent service that is focused on the needs of children in the transition between primary and secondary school whose parents would normally find the admissions system harder to navigate. Local authorities should be creative about using a range of media to reach these parents, for example, through targeted communications, admissions fairs, and group or one-to-one sessions as appropriate. Guidelines for local authorities on the provision of Choice Advice are provided at Appendix 5.

1.7 This Code provides admission authorities with considerable flexibility to determine and implement their own admission arrangements in order to meet local circumstances, whilst providing a clear framework to ensure that unlawful and unfair arrangements are not adopted and that the needs of all children are met.

Duties to increase opportunities for parental choice, respond to parental representations, and improve community cohesion

1.8 Following commencement of the relevant provisions of the Education and Inspections Act 2006, local authorities will be required to promote fair access to educational opportunity, promote high standards and the fulfilment by every child of his educational potential, secure choice and diversity and respond to parental representations. These new duties, together with this Code, will underpin a modernised role for local authorities as the commissioners of school education, ensuring the quality of provision for all in a system that is responsive to the needs of parents and children. The Education and Inspections Act 2006 places new duties on local authorities as set out in paragraphs 1.9 to 1.13 below.

1.9 Section 13A of the Education Act 1996 (as inserted by Section 1 of the Education and Inspections Act 2006) requires local authorities to exercise their functions with a view to promoting the fulfilment by every child of his educational potential, and, in the case of local education authorities in England, with a view to ensuring fair access to educational opportunity, as well as with a view to promoting high standards.

1.10 Local authorities have a new statutory duty under section 14(3A) of the Education Act 1996 (as inserted by Section 2 of the Education and Inspections Act 2006) to secure diversity and increase opportunities for parental choice when planning the provision of school places.

1.11 In addition, local authorities **must** consider parental representations about the provision of schools in their areas and respond setting out any action which the authority proposes to take, or where the authority believes no action is necessary, their reasons behind that opinion. Local authorities **must** determine how to carry out these new duties in the light of their local circumstances and in accordance with guidance issued by the Secretary of State under section 14A of the Education Act 1996 (as inserted by Section 3 of the Education and Inspections Act 2006).

1.12 Local authorities **should** be able to show how their strategic planning functions take into account these new statutory duties.

1.13 Furthermore, Governing Bodies of all maintained schools **must** promote community cohesion, under section 21 of the Education Act 2002 as amended by section 38 of the Education and Inspections Act 2006. Ofsted will report on the discharge of this duty[8].

Admissions: key statutory provisions

1.14 The key statutory provisions relating to school admissions are shown below. Admission authorities **must** also comply with other legislation relevant to school admissions such as those included in Appendix 1.

Admission arrangements for Academies

1.15 These are approved by the Secretary of State as part of an Academy's funding agreement, which requires it to comply with admissions legislation and relevant Codes. An Academy **must** consult annually in the same way as other admission authorities do, but **must not** alter its admission arrangements without the approval of the Secretary of State. Any objections to an Academy's admission arrangements will be considered by the Secretary of State.

---

[8] Section 5 of the EA 2005 as amended by section 154 of the EIA 2006

Co-ordinated admission schemes

1.16 All local authorities are required, by regulations[9] made under sections 89B and 89C of the School Standards and Framework Act 1998, to formulate and consult on a scheme for each academic year for co-ordinating admission arrangements for all maintained schools within their area. This requirement includes maintained boarding schools, but excludes maintained special schools and maintained nursery schools. Co-ordination schemes are intended to simplify the admission process for parents whilst reducing the likelihood of any child being left without a school place. Co-ordination establishes a mechanism that ensures that, as far as is practical, every child living in a local authority area who has applied in the normal admissions round receives one, and only one, offer of a school place on the same day[10]. While it is for each local authority to decide the scheme that best suits its residents and its schools, they **must** ensure that they:

a)   comply with law and regulations, including all the process requirements (for example, the common application form allowing at least 3 preferences, information sharing with other local authorities, sending out not more than one offer to all seeking secondary places at its maintained schools or Academies on the same day); and

b)   do not disadvantage applications to their schools from families resident in other local authorities (which would be contrary to the Greenwich Judgment[11]).

1.17 Co-ordination schemes do not affect the rights and duties of the governing bodies of voluntary aided and foundation schools to set and apply their own admission arrangements and oversubscription criteria. Admission authorities do not have to determine the same or similar oversubscription criteria, but **must** ensure that their own admission arrangements are compatible with, and do not undermine, the co-ordination scheme for their area. Full details of how the co-ordination scheme works **must** be included in the local authority's composite prospectus[12] (see Appendix 4).

---

[9] The School Admission (Co-ordination of Admissions Arrangements) (England) Regulations 2007 (SI 2007/194)

[10] For primary schools, this is the day that is published in their admission arrangements; for secondary schools, this is the national offer date (1 March or next working day).

[11] R v Greenwich London Borough Council, ex parte John Ball Primary School (1989) 88 LGR 589 [1990] Fam Law 469

[12] The Education (School Information) (England) Regulations 2002 (SI 2002/2897), as amended by SI 2005/2152

1.18   Academies are required by their funding agreements to participate in co-ordination schemes and local authorities **must** consult them, as well as other admission authorities, in order to agree the scheme. Local authorities **must** also invite City Technology Colleges to participate in the scheme.

1.19   If a local authority does not notify the Secretary of State that it has adopted a co-ordination scheme by 15 April each year, the Secretary of State may impose one[13].

Admission numbers

1.20   A school **must** have an admission number for each 'relevant age group'. This is defined in law as "an age group in which pupils are or will normally be admitted" to the school in question[14]. It may be necessary for some schools to have more than one admission number. Where a secondary school operates a sixth form and admits children from other schools at age 16, for instance, an admission number will be required for year 12 as well as for the main year or years in which children join the lower school. Admission numbers **must** refer in each case to children to be admitted to the school for the first time. They **must not** include children transferring from earlier age groups, except where in the case of a primary school making nursery provision, the admission number will be the number of all children to be admitted to the reception year, and including children who may have attended the nursery (whose parents must make separate applications for places in reception). Maintained boarding schools may set separate admission numbers for day places and boarding places, for each year that they intend to admit children.

---

[13] The School Admission (Co-ordination of Admissions Arrangements) (England) Regulations 2007 (SI 2007/194)
[14] Section 142 of the SSFA 1998

1.21 Admission authorities **must** set admission numbers with regard to the capacity assessment for the school[15]. Admission authorities may fix an admission number for a relevant age group that is lower than the capacity assessment. If they do so, they **must** publish this information for parents at the same time as they notify the bodies they are required to consult about the determination of their admission arrangements, who may object to the admission number. They can also set a higher admission number than that indicated by the capacity assessment. In relation to admission numbers applicable to infant classes, the admission number **must** be compatible with the duty to comply with the infant class size limit[16] (see paragraph 2.57). Admission authorities are required to consult before setting or amending a published admission number. Once an admission number has been set by the admission authority, children **should not** be admitted above the published number unless exceptional circumstances apply or as part of in-year fair access protocols (see Chapter 3) or a closing school (see paragraph 1.40).

1.22 Section 98 of the School Standards and Framework Act 1998[17] requires that children with statements of special educational needs admitted during a normal admission round to a relevant age group **must** be taken into account when determining and applying a school's admission number. Accordingly, children with statements already admitted to a school **must** be counted towards the admission number when considering whether there is still a place available for another child without a statement.

1.23 Section 86(5)[18] of the School Standards and Framework Act 1998 requires that in a normal year of entry, a child **must not** be refused admission to a school on the grounds of prejudice to efficient education or the efficient use of resources except where the number of applications for admission exceeds the admission number. Although there is an expectation that this admission number will continue to be applied as that year group progresses through school, it is permissible to refuse admission to it if circumstances have changed since it was a 'relevant age group' and admission of an additional child would 'prejudice the provision of efficient education or the efficient use of resources'.

---

[15] The Education (Determination of Admission Arrangements) Regulations 1999 (SI 1999/126) as amended by SI 2002/2896 and SI 2007/497

[16] Section 1 of the SSFA 1998

[17] As amended by paragraph 12 of Schedule 4 to the 2002 Act

[18] As substituted by section 47 of the 2002 Act

Consultation

1.24   Consultation is an important part of the process of formulating and determining admission arrangements, and local authorities and admission authorities **must** work together to ensure that schools' arrangements meet the needs of all parents and children. It is good practice for local authorities to co-ordinate consultation in their areas. All admission authorities are required[19] to complete their consultation by 1 March, and determine their arrangements by the 15 April, in each calendar year for the following school year[20] (unless an exception applies – see paragraph 3 of appendix 4). The governing bodies of Academies are also required, by their funding agreements, to consult on their admission arrangements. Additional guidelines on consultation can be found in Appendix 4.

Duty to publish and follow determined admission arrangements and consequences of not doing so

1.25   Local authorities are required by section 92 of the School Standards and Framework Act 1998 and the Education (School Information) (England) Regulations 2002[21] to publish in hard copy, the admission arrangements for all maintained schools and Academies in their area and make this information available for parents. Admission authorities **must** then follow the determined, published admission arrangements. Failure to do so would amount to a breach of the admission authority's statutory duty.

---

[19] Section 89(2) of the SSFA 1998. These dates are prescribed in The Education (Determination of Admission Arrangements) Regulations 1999 (SI 1999/126) as amended by SI 2002/ 2896 and SI 2007/497

[20] For example, for the 2008 school year admission authorities must have completed consultation by 1 March 2007 and determined by 15 April 2007

[21] The Education (School Information) (England) Regulations 2002 (SI 2002/2897) as amended by SI 2005/2152. Regulation 8 and Schedule 2 of these Regulations also require the composite prospectus to include oversubscription criteria for all schools in the area and the admission number. For secondary schools, the prospectus must include details of the number of applicants in the previous year.

1.26 Under section 88(1A) of the School Standards and Framework Act 1998 (as inserted by section 43 of the Education and Inspections Act 2006), it is the duty of a governing body of a community or voluntary controlled school, for which a local authority is the admissions authority, to implement any decision relating to the admission of children taken by the admission authority. Similarly, under section 89C(3A) of the School Standards and Framework Act 1998 and regulations, the governing body of a voluntary aided or foundation school **must** implement a decision of the local authority, made in accordance with the relevant area's co-ordinated admission scheme, to admit a child to the school.

1.27 Failure to comply with a statutory requirement or any proposal to use unlawful arrangements can be referred to the Secretary of State who may use his powers under section 497 of the Education Act 1996 to make a direction to enforce the statutory requirement or prevent an unlawful act.

Considering applications for school places

1.28 All admission authorities **must** consider and decide on applications for school places in accordance with their published arrangements. If a school is undersubscribed then all applications **must** be accepted, unless applicants do not meet minimum academic standards set for entry to a grammar school or sixth form.

1.29 If a school is oversubscribed then the admission authority **must** consider all applicants against its published oversubscription criteria. Guidelines for admission authorities on admissions outside the normal admission round (which covers both in-year admissions and admissions at the start of a school year which is not a normal year of admission to the school) are provided in chapter 3.

Complying with parental preferences

1.30 Parents have a right to express a preference for a place in any maintained school, City Technology College or Academy. The statutory duty under section 86 of the School Standards and Framework Act 1998 to comply with parental preferences is not affected by co-ordinated admission arrangements. Where more than one place could be offered under the co-ordination scheme, the duty to comply applies to the single offer that is to be made in accordance with the arrangements in the scheme, and not any other possible offers. Schools **must not** inform parents of any possible offers – only the local authority can convey the single offer.

1.31 Co-ordination schemes **must** state the mechanism to be used to decide which place will be offered in the event that offers could be made at two or more schools. Local authorities **must** ensure in their schemes that parents will receive their highest available preference. If none of the parent's preferences is available the scheme **must** say clearly how a place at another school will be allocated. Another school **must** be allocated unless there are insufficient places remaining in the local authority; in this case, all remaining places **must** be allocated so that a minimum number of children are without the offer of a school place. Local authorities **must** also set out in their schemes how late applications, and arrangements for admissions outside the normal admissions round, will be handled (see chapter 3). Local authorities **must** ensure that the admissions process is co-ordinated beyond offer date. Local authorities and Admission Forums **should** also consider how the in-year admissions process could be better co-ordinated so that local authorities are aware of pupil movement into and around their area, and so that children spend the minimum necessary time out of school.

1.32 Further guidelines on the statutory basis for co-ordinated admission schemes, including the key obligations placed on local authorities by the regulations, are set out in Appendix 3.

1.33 Once parents have made their preferences, local authorities **must not** allow them to be changed without a genuine reason for doing so, for example, if the family has recently moved address. Local authorities **must** make this clear in the information they provide for parents.

1.34 Where parents are unsuccessful in applying for a school place for their child, they **must** be given reasons and informed in writing of their right to an independent appeal against the decision.

Applications for Year 12 entry and transfer from Year 11

1.35. The admission authorities for schools with a sixth form **must** consult on and determine the arrangements they propose to use to allocate places in Year 12 at the same time as other admission arrangements[22]. As with admissions at compulsory school age, parental preference **must** be met (where possible)[23] and the admission authority **must** act in accordance with this Code and take account of the advice of the Admission Forum[24]. Applicants refused admission are entitled to appeal to an independent appeal panel[25].

1.36 An admission number need only be set for sixth form when it is a normal point of entry to the school, i.e. the school sets out to admit external candidates to its sixth form, rather than just to deal with ad-hoc applications. While it is good practice to say in published information what the anticipated sixth form intake will be (taking into account both internal and external candidates), the published admission number **must** relate only to those being admitted to the school for the first time, and **should** be based on an estimate of the minimum number of external candidates likely to be admitted, although it would be acceptable to exceed this if demand for available courses can be met.

1.37 It is not necessary for children already in the school to apply formally for places in Year 12, but the admission arrangements **must** give details of any entry requirements (such as minimum entry qualifications, which can include a level of attainment at GCSE and **must** be the same as the criteria for external applicants) and oversubscription criteria. Schools **must not** interview children or their families for entry to Year 12, although meetings can be held to provide advice on options and entry requirements for particular courses. Entry **must not** be dependent on attendance, behaviour record, or perceptions of attitude or motivation. Any applicant refused a place in Year 12 is entitled to make an appeal to an independent appeal panel, whether the child is already attending the school or is an external candidate.

---

[22] Sections 89 and 89A of the SSFA 1998
[23] Section 86(3A) and (3B) of the SSFA 1998 as inserted by paragraph 3 of Schedule 4 to the 2002 Act
[24] Section 84(3) and 85A(4) of the SSFA 1998
[25] Section 94(1) and (1A) of the SSFA 1998

1.38 If admission authorities are to set criteria for transfer or admission to the sixth form based on ability, they **should** take into account the needs of the children and the provision of suitable post-compulsory education available in the area that a child would have access to if they failed to meet the criteria. Many schools still offer only academic courses in Year 12, and it would be reasonable for them to require applicants to have a specified number of GCSEs at particular grades. However, a growing number of schools now offer a wider range of courses, which make it impracticable to set the same entry requirements. In these cases, it would be acceptable to state what courses are available, the entry requirements for each, and how priority for entry to these courses will be determined if they are oversubscribed.

Admission to new schools

1.39 Full details of proposed admission arrangements, as prescribed by regulations[26], **must** be set out in statutory proposals for new schools. Once approved, they **must** remain unchanged for two years after the first year of operation unless the Schools Adjudicator allows an application to vary them because of a major change of circumstances.

Closing schools

1.40 While a merger or replacement of a school by another school or an Academy often results in children transferring to the roll of the replacement or merged school, the situation is different when a school is not replaced and children transfer to different schools. In these circumstances the local authority **must** collaborate with all schools in an area to consider the best way of securing provision for children at the closing school. Where it has not been feasible to manage a school's closure over a transitional period i.e. stopping new admissions and continuing with existing pupils, the following are good practices which have been successfully adopted:

a)   The local authority identifies schools with places available, negotiating with them and other schools which may be able to help, then offers places to children from the closing school.

b)   The local authority carries out a preference exercise with parents of children on roll at the closing school, considering their preferences and, where necessary, negotiating with schools to provide additional places. In these circumstances, it is acceptable to give precedence to these children over any on waiting lists (see paragraphs 3.26 to 3.28) and, along with

---

[26] School Organisation (Establishment and Discontinuance of Schools)(England) Regulations 2007

admitting in accordance with an in-year fair access protocol (see paragraphs 3.14 to 3.19), to admit above the school's published admission number.

1.41   In the scenarios above, parents still have a statutory right to apply for a place at any school, with a right of appeal if refused a place at any of their preferred schools.

Entry on school roll

1.42   A child **must** be included in a school's Admission Register from the beginning of the first day on which the school has agreed, or has been notified, that the children will attend the school[27]. In the case of admission to community or voluntary controlled schools, the local authority **should** notify the school of the date by which the child is to be admitted so that there is no ambiguity about the date from which the child is on the school roll.

Withdrawing offers of places

1.43   Once an offer of a school place has been made through the co-ordinated scheme, it is only reasonable for an admission authority to withdraw that offer in very limited circumstances. These may include when a parent has failed to respond to an offer within a reasonable time or the admission authority offered the place on the basis of a fraudulent or intentionally misleading application from a parent (for example, a false claim to residence in a catchment area) which effectively denied a place to a child with a stronger claim; or where a place was offered by the local authority, not the admission authority, in error. If a parent has not responded to the offer of a place within a reasonable time (such as 21 days), the admission authority **must** remind the parent of the need to respond and point out that the place may be withdrawn if they do not.

1.44   A school place **must not** be withdrawn once a child has started at the school, except where that place was fraudulently obtained. In deciding whether to withdraw the place, the length of time that the child had been at the school **must** be taken into account. Where a place is withdrawn on the basis of misleading information, the application **must** be considered afresh, and a right of appeal offered if a place is refused.

---

[27] The Education (Pupil Registration) Regulations 2006 (SI 2006/1751)

1.45 A decision to refuse admission **must not** be made by one individual in a school. Where the school is its own admission authority the whole governing body, or an admissions committee established by the governing body, **must** make such decisions[28]. Head teachers or other school officials **must not** give parents an expectation that their application will be successful, or tell them that their child has been given a place at the school, before an offer of a place has been made formally under the co-ordinated scheme. Case law has established that where there is evidence that parents have been told by a head teacher, or other school official, that their child will be given a place at a school, they can reasonably expect that the person making the offer had authority to do so. In these circumstances the admission authority **should** normally honour the offer, even though in fact it may not have authorised that person to make it.

Interviewing

1.46 Section 88A of the School Standards and Framework Act 1998 (as inserted by section 44 of the Education and Inspections Act 2006) prohibits the interviewing of parents and/or children as a method for deciding whether a child is to be offered a place at a school. Admission authorities **must not** use either face-to-face interviews or interviews by telephone or other means. Open days, meetings to discuss options, and other events for prospective parents and children are not affected (see guidelines in paragraph 1.70).

1.47 This prohibition does not apply to interviews conducted by boarding schools solely for the purpose of assessing a child's suitability for a boarding place, or to auditions or other oral or practical tests in order to ascertain a child's aptitude in a particular subject at schools with a permitted form of selection by aptitude in accordance with section 99(4) of the School Standards and Framework Act 1998.

Selection by ability

1.48 Section 39 of the Education and Inspections Act 2006, which re-states section 99 of the School Standards and Framework Act 1998, prohibits the introduction of any new selection by ability, other than for banding (see paragraphs 2.77 to 2.84) or for sixth forms. Only grammar schools or schools with partially selective arrangements which already had such arrangements in place during the 1997-98 school year are permitted to continue to use selection by ability, if unchanged since that school year. Additional guidelines on permitted forms of selection are included in Chapter 2.

---

[28] The School Governance (Procedures) (England) Regulations 2003 (SI 2003/1377)

Home–school agreements

1.49 Admission to a school **must not** be conditional on parents signing a home–school agreement, under section 111 of the School Standards and Framework Act 1998. Home-school agreements are a useful means of promoting greater involvement by parents in their children's education. However, schools **must not** ask parents to sign agreements before they have been offered a place at the school. Further guidance is available in the 'Home-School Agreements: Guidance for schools'[29].

Statements of Special Educational Needs

1.50 Section 324 of the Education Act 1996 requires the governing bodies of all maintained schools to admit a child with a statement of special educational needs that names their school. More detailed information and guidelines on the law in relation to children with special educational needs are provided in paragraph 3.17.

Children in public care (looked after children/children in care)

1.51 A child in public care (looked after child)[30], is a child who is in the care of a local authority or provided with accommodation by that authority. In this Code we refer to these children as 'children in care'. Admission authorities are required to give highest priority to children in care in their oversubscription criteria. More detailed guidelines on children in care are provided in Chapter 2.

Children from overseas

1.52 Parents who are living in England, and whose children have accompanied them, may express a preference for their children to attend a maintained school under the normal admission arrangements described in this Code. This includes the children of asylum seekers; parents who have limited leave to enter or remain in the UK; and teachers coming to the UK with their children on a teacher exchange scheme.

1.53 However, different rules operate in relation to those making applications from overseas as set out below.

---

[29] 'Home–Schools Agreements: Guidance for Schools', DfES, 1998 (www.dfes.gov.uk/hsa)

[30] This means a child who is looked after by a local authority in accordance with section 22 of the Children Act 1989

British citizens and lone children with right of abode

1.54 There are no restrictions on entry to the UK for children (whether or not accompanied by their parents) who hold full British Citizen passports (but not British Dependent Territories or British Overseas passports) or children from countries whose passports have been endorsed to show that they have the right of abode in this country. Such children will be permitted to enter this country irrespective of their purpose in doing so and are entitled to apply for a place at a maintained school.

EEA nationals

1.55 Under European Community law, and where the provisions of the Immigration (European Economic Area) Regulations 2006 are satisfied, nationals of the European Economic Area (which comprises the all member states of the European Union together with Iceland, Norway and Liechtenstein) and their children of any age, who come to the UK lawfully to work or for certain other economic purposes have a right to reside in the UK. They enjoy the same rights to education as British citizens. This applies equally to lone EEA national children who come to the UK as students, who are not accompanied by their parents. Non-EEA children of EEA parents who are not accompanied by their parents do not have this right.

Non-EEA nationals

1.56 Non-EEA children who apply for leave to enter or remain in the UK to study on their own will only be granted leave to enter or remain if the child satisfies the requirements specified in paragraph 57 of the Immigration Rules[31]. If the child is less than 16 years old, he or she must produce proof of acceptance for a course of study at an independent fee-paying school outside the maintained sector or a bona fide private educational institution. The child will not be allowed to enter to attend a maintained school, except as part of an exchange programme. If such a child is found to attend a maintained school they will infringe the conditions of their leave to enter and action could be taken against them by the Immigration and Nationality Directorate of the Home Office.

---

[31] The Immigration Rules can be viewed on www.ind.homeoffice.gov.uk

1.57 However, whilst non-EEA overseas students are not, in general, admitted to this country to attend maintained schools, these students can be admitted to attend a maintained school under the auspices of a student exchange scheme, or if they are participants in the EU Lifelong Learning Programme. A student participating in such schemes will not be permitted to stay in this country for more than one year. Unless as part of the EU Lifelong Learning Programme or its successors, such schemes **must** include a genuine exchange of students between partner schools at the same time or a later date, and **should not** involve fees. Where a child on roll at a UK maintained school participates in a student exchange scheme that child **should** remain on roll for the duration of the exchange and be treated as on an "approved educational activity".

Other applicants

1.58 Holders of passports describing them as British Dependent Territories Citizens or British Overseas Citizens have no automatic right of abode in the UK, nor do other non-EEA nationals. They and their dependent children are in the same position as those described in paragraphs 1.56 and 1.57.

Teacher exchange schemes

1.59 Where a child goes abroad to accompany his or her parent on a teacher exchange scheme, the school **should** ensure that the child is able to take up his or her place on return. The child remains on roll and time away may be treated as an "approved educational activity".

1.60 The local authority has a duty to find a place for a child who will become resident in their area as a result of his or her parent's participation in a teacher exchange scheme. Local authorities **should** plan in advance for the needs of these children to ensure that they can take up a suitable school place for the duration of the exchange, wherever this is practicable.

Maintained boarding schools

1.61 The same immigration and school admission rules apply as regards admission to a maintained boarding school. Such schools may charge boarding fees but they cannot charge tuition fees. Children without the right of abode will not be allowed to enter the country to attend maintained boarding schools (see paragraph 1.58).

1.62 As noted above, lone children may be admitted to the UK if they can show that they have a place at an independent, fee-paying school. Where a child has been given leave to enter on that basis, the Home Office will not normally grant an extension of stay, or amend the child's conditions of entry, if the child transfers to a maintained school or Academy. Local authorities and governing bodies may wish to bear this in mind when considering a request for a transfer in respect of a child from overseas who has been previously attending a fee-paying school.

Applications made in the UK for children living abroad

1.63 Admission authorities may receive an application from parents overseas for a school place for a child who is not yet resident in the UK. The admission authority will not necessarily know when the child is expected to be resident in the UK, or whether a parent's application for leave to enter the UK has been or will be successful, or if it has been, on what terms entry has been granted. These are all considerations that an admission authority may reasonably wish to take into account when considering the application.

Ensuring equity and fair access

1.64 Local authorities are required by section 13A of the Education Act 1996 (as substituted by section 1 of the Education and Inspections Act 2006) to ensure fair access to educational opportunity and this duty applies to a wide range of education functions. Local authorities **must** consider, for example, whether their admission or transport policies, their extended services provision or local funding formulae are in line with the principle of fair access to educational opportunity.

1.65 Parents must be able to make informed decisions when applying for school places for their children. The admissions system can appear very complex to some parents and admission authorities **must** make every effort to ensure that all parents are able to understand the process and in particular how oversubscription criteria will be applied. Parents should also have access to all relevant information before they make their application. It is easier for parents to understand local admissions systems that are clear, objective and fair. Above all, parents need to be able to understand whether they have a realistic chance of being offered a place for their child at any particular school. In drawing up their admission arrangements, admission authorities **must** ensure that the practices and the criteria used to decide the allocation of school places:

a) are clear in the sense of being free from doubt and easily understood. Arrangements that are vague only lead to uncertainty and this may reduce the ability of parents to make an informed choice for their children. They are also likely to increase the chances of an objection;

b) are objective and based on known facts. Admission authorities and governing bodies **must not** make subjective decisions or use subjective criteria;

c) are procedurally fair and are also equitable for all groups of children (including those with special educational needs, disabilities, those in public care, or who may be a young carer);

d) enable parents' preferences for the schools of their choice to be met to the maximum extent possible;

e) provide parents or carers with easy access to helpful admissions information. (Regulations[32] require the local authority to produce a composite prospectus that covers admission arrangements for all schools in their area. See Appendix 4);

f) comply with all relevant legislation, including on infant class sizes and on equal opportunities, and have been determined in accordance with the statutory requirements and the mandatory provisions of this Code.

1.66 Admission authorities **must** consult each other and co-ordinate their arrangements, including over the rapid re-integration of children including those who have been excluded from other schools and who arrive in an area after the normal admissions round (see Chapter 3), in accordance with local in-year fair access protocols for securing schools for unplaced children (see paragraphs 3.14 to 3.19).

---

[32] The Education (School Information) (England) Regulations 2002 (SI 2002 /2897), as amended by SI 2005/2152.

Ensuring fair access - Implications of wider policies

1.67   Admission authorities and governing bodies **must** ensure that their admission arrangements and other school policies are fair and do not disadvantage, either directly or indirectly, a child from a particular social or racial group, or a child with a disability or special educational needs. Local authorities and schools have duties under Part 4 of the Disability Discrimination Act 1995 not to discriminate against disabled children and this is an important principle that should underpin all schools' policies, not just admissions. Admission authorities **must** also ensure that their admission arrangements comply with all other relevant equalities legislation (see Appendix 1). Admission authorities and governing bodies **should** develop and implement admission arrangements, practices and oversubscription criteria that actively promote equity, and thus go further than simply ensuring that unfair practices and criteria are excluded.

1.68   All governing bodies **must** ensure that their other policies and practices do not disadvantage certain social groups or discourage some groups of parents from seeking a place at the school for their child. Local authorities **must** work with governing bodies (where the governing body is not also the admission authority) to ensure that admission arrangements which appear fair are not then undermined by other school policies, such as a requirement for expensive school uniform, sportswear or expensive school trips or other activities, unless arrangements are put in place to ensure that parents on low incomes can afford them. Governing bodies of schools which are their own admission authority need to address this too. Guidelines on some of these issues are set out below.

1.69   Admission authorities and governing bodies **should** also guard against any conflicts of interest for those who make decisions about applications that could leave them open to challenges, for example declaring personal knowledge of a particular child or friendship with their family.

Practices and policies that may undermine fair admission arrangements
Information about parents, children and families

1.70   The use of interviews in school admission arrangements is unlawful (see paragraphs 1.46 and 1.47). Staff and governors are encouraged to meet parents at open evenings and on other occasions, but information gained in this way **must not** play a part in the admission decision-making process. Attendance at an open evening or other meeting at the school **must not** be a condition for the allocation of a place.

Applications and application forms

Prohibition of supplementary forms

1.71 Admission authorities **must not** use supplementary application or information forms that ask:

a) for any personal details about parents, such as criminal convictions or marital, occupational or financial status;

b) for details about parents' achievements, educational background or whether their first language is English;

c) for details about parents' or children's disabilities, special educational needs or medical conditions, unless this is in support of positive action as described in Chapters 2 and 3;

d) about parents' or children's interests, hobbies or membership of societies (this does not apply to membership or participation in activities as part of religious observance or practice at schools designated as having a religious character).

1.72 Admission authorities **must not** discriminate against children whose parents fall into certain social groups. No personal information about parents is relevant in considering an application for a place at a school and criteria which focus on parents cannot legitimately be included as oversubscription criteria. Collecting such information may suggest that it can be taken into account and therefore be misleading to parents.

1.73 Given the potential for discrimination, admission authorities may only use supplementary application/information forms that request additional information when it has a direct bearing on decisions about acceptable oversubscription criteria; for example, asking for a reference from a priest or other religious minister for a school designated as having a religious character (faith school) or to assess an application for a boarding place.

Boarding Schools

1.74 This Code applies to all maintained schools including those with boarding places. In considering applications for boarding places schools **must** comply with the law and the mandatory requirements of this Code and follow its guidelines. The prohibition at 1.71 does not prevent schools with boarding places from using supplementary information forms to establish a child's suitability for boarding or to collect information necessary in order to consider an application against their published oversubscription criteria (see paragraph 2.54). Boarding schools **must not** use supplementary information forms or interviews in considering applications for day places or ask for any of the information listed in paragraph 1.71 for day or boarding places. Guidelines on setting oversubscription criteria for boarding places are provided at paragraphs 2.54 to 2.55 and guidelines on assessing suitability for boarding are at Appendix 6.

1.75 Schools with boarding places **must** determine their oversubscription criteria in accordance with the mandatory provisions and guidelines set out in Chapter 2 of this Code, and **must not** adopt suitability for boarding as an oversubscription criterion. Any boarding school wishing to assess suitability **must** make it clear in its admission arrangements how it intends to do so for all boarding applicants prior to applying its oversubscription criteria.

Faith schools (schools designated by the Secretary of State as having a religious character – referred to in this Code as faith schools)

1.76 At faith schools, the prohibition in paragraph 1.71 does not prevent the use of a supplementary form that asks parents or children about their membership of or relationship with the church or religious denomination in accordance with paragraphs 2.41 to 2.53 of this Code.

Entry tests, application forms and photographs

1.77 Unless part of approved aptitude selection or banding arrangements (see paragraphs 2.72 to 2.84), tests **must not** be used by non-selective schools as a means of allocating places at the school.

1.78 Photographs of children may be used only by schools that use tests and then only as a security measure to verify that the child presenting for the test is the child named on the application. Otherwise, photographs **must not** be required with applications for school places.

1.79 Applications and any permitted supplementary forms **must** be completed by parents or carers; admission authorities **must not** ask children to complete application forms for school places.

Other policies

School uniform

1.80 School uniform plays a valuable role in contributing to the ethos and setting the tone of a school, and the Government strongly encourages schools to consider the introduction of uniforms where they do not already have them. Governing bodies **should** help limit the expense of uniforms so that parents on low incomes do not feel that the prospective cost of the uniform means that they cannot apply for their preferred school. Governing bodies **should** ensure that the uniform chosen is widely available in high street shops and other retail outlets, and internet suppliers rather than from an expensive sole supplier. They can use their own purchasing power to buy in bulk and pass on savings to parents. Governing bodies **should not** seek to operate as sole suppliers in order to raise additional funds through the sale of new school uniforms.

1.81 All schools which have a uniform policy **should** have arrangements in place to ensure that no family feels unable to apply for admission on account of high uniform costs. This applies equally to sports kits and any other specialist equipment outlined in the policy. Schemes for remission of cost **should** cover children eligible for free school meals, and children whose parents are entitled to the maximum level of working tax credit. Schemes **should** be administered discreetly so that no parent is embarrassed to ask for help. These schemes **should** be widely publicised and clearly explained in admissions, or other, literature provided by the school[33].

Contributions to school funds and contributions to participate in school trips

1.82 Admission authorities and governing bodies **must** make it clear in their admission arrangements that there is no charge or cost related to the admission of a child to a school. Schools **should not** imply in their prospectus and in other documents that donations and voluntary contributions are expected. Parents from low-income families sometimes express concern about the level of voluntary contributions that schools request or require and may be deterred by these from expressing a preference for the school for their child.

---

[33] Further guidance on school uniforms can be accessed at:
www.parentscentre.co.uk/educationandlearning/schoollife/schooladministration/uniforms

1.83 School trips are an important part of school life and can contribute to the ethos of the school. However, some parents may not want their children to go away from home or to take part in school trips. Governing bodies **must not** imply that such trips are compulsory and as a result discourage some parents from applying for a place at the school.

1.84 Parents may also be concerned about the cost of school trips and other extra-curricular activities, fearing that their child may not be able to participate and this may discourage them from applying for a place at the school. Accordingly, schools **should** make it clear where help may be available for those unable to afford the cost of school trips. They **must** make it clear that any contribution to school funds and voluntary contributions to trips are not mandatory, and that the expectation is that low income families will contribute a small amount, or nothing. Parents **must** be assured that they will not be asked to explain why they prefer not to contribute and that not contributing will in no way disadvantage their child.

1.85 A charge **must not** be made for a school trip[34]:

a) that is during school hours; or

b) is outside school hours but it is being undertaken as part of the National Curriculum, or as part of a syllabus for a prescribed public examination.

1.86 A charge may be made for board and lodging on residential trips but the charge **must not** exceed the actual cost, and children in receipt of free school meals are exempt. Schools may, however, ask for voluntary contributions towards the cost of board and lodging.

---

[34] The EA 1996 (Sections 449-462), as amended by the SSFA 1998 and the EA 2002 , sets out the legislative basis for school charging and remissions policies. Section 200 of the EA 2002 amended the legislation that deals with the remission of charges (board and lodgings) for residential school trips, set out in section 457 of the EA 1996. The Education (School Sessions and Charges and Remissions Policies)(Information)(England) Regulations 1999, (SI 1999/ 2255), places obligations on head teachers, school governing bodies and LEAs to make information available about charging and remissions policies.

School transport

1.87 The cost and availability of safe, reliable home to school transport is a concern
for many parents. Home to school travel arrangements can have a
disproportionate impact on low-income families, particularly those with several
children. Admission authorities **must** explain clearly whether or not school
transport will be available and, if so, to which schools and at what cost (if any).
Local authorities **must** make information about school travel and transport
options available to parents at least six weeks before parents apply for a school
place[35]. The Education and Inspections Act 2006 extends rights to free home to
school transport to maintained schools and Academies for children from low
income families (defined as those whose children are entitled to free school
meals or who are in receipt of their maximum level of Working Tax Credit).
This will remove the lack of affordable transport as a barrier to choice for these
families. Admission authorities **must** bring this information to the attention of
parents. The position is different for primary and secondary schools:

a) for children of primary age, transport will only be provided to the nearest
suitable school, but for those in low income families aged 8–11, local
authorities **must** ensure that free transport is provided for children living
more than two miles from the school.

b) for children of secondary age, local authorities **must** ensure that those from
low income families have free transport to any one of the three nearest
suitable schools, where the distance traveled is between two and six miles.
Local authorities **must** also ensure that transport is provided to the nearest
school preferred on the grounds of religion or belief[36] where this is between
2 and 15 miles away.

---

[35] The Education School Information (England) Regulations 2002(SI 2002/2897), as amended by (SI
2005/2152)
[36] As defined by Part 2 of the Equality Act 2006

Extended schools

1.88 For children and young people to attain their full potential, they and their families need access to a wide range of opportunities to help overcome the barriers which many of them face – especially those of poverty, disadvantage and disability. Many schools are already offering, or developing, such opportunities. The Government wants all schools to develop access to extended opportunities. The five 'core' services are described in 'Extended Schools: Access to opportunities and services for all'[37] although schools are also free to offer other opportunities as well, where they identify unmet local needs.

1.89 It is important that schools ensure access to extended activities, where they may be of educational benefit, for children and young people whose families cannot afford to pay for them; and therefore that they do not discourage disadvantaged families from applying for a place at the school, through fear that their child may not be able to participate in extended activities. All schools should be able to provide some free study support for children and young people from disadvantaged backgrounds through the flexibility in their delegated budgets and their School Standards Grant. Schools may also use their delegated budgets and their School Standards Grant to support access for these children and young people to educational activities which are normally included as part of a childcare offer, although they are not participating in the childcare.

Being proactive about promoting equity and extending opportunity for all

1.90 It is good practice for admission authorities to analyse information on their intakes, and where possible their applicants, to find out whether they attract a wide range of families or whether their school fails to attract all sections of the local community. However, any survey undertaken to gather such information **must not** be connected to decisions about admissions and **should** only be undertaken after children have been admitted.

1.91 Admission authorities for all schools **must** act upon any information that suggests that the school's or admission authority's policies or practices appear to be unfairly disadvantaging one group of children compared to another. There are many ways in which this might be done, for example, the most popular schools might work with primary schools in more deprived areas to encourage applications from poorer families.

---

[37] www.teachernet.gov.uk/extendedschools

Admission forums

1.92 Admission Forums have an important role in monitoring compliance with the provisions of this Code, and the overall impact of the admission arrangements of schools in an area on fair access. All Forums have a power to produce an annual report. The Education (Admission Forums) (England) Regulations 2002[38] set out a full list of matters to be covered including information on the number of preferences met and the social and ethnic mix of schools compared with the communities they serve. Admission authorities and schools that are found to be using practices or oversubscription criteria that work against fair access are likely to be failing in their duty to act in accordance with the provisions of this Code. Local authorities, other local schools, the Admissions Forum and parents all have important roles to play in ensuring fairness: more detailed guidelines on monitoring and enforcing this Code are provided in Chapter 4.

---

[38] As amended by SI 2007/192.

Chapter 2

Setting Fair Oversubscription Criteria

This chapter provides guidelines and imposes mandatory requirements on setting fair oversubscription criteria:

- **Children with statements of special educational needs (2.6)**

- **Children in care (looked after children) (2.7)**

- **Prohibition of unfair oversubscription criteria (2.13)**

- **Guidelines on setting fair oversubscription criteria (2.15)**

    - **Giving priority to siblings (2.17)**

    - **Social and medical need (2.24)**

    - **Random allocation (2.28)**

    - **Distance and ease of access by public transport (2.31)**

    - **Catchment areas (2.35)**

- **Additional guidelines for faith schools (2.41)**

- **Additional guidelines for boarding schools (2.54)**

- **Additional guidelines for primary schools (2.56)**

    - **Infant Classes (2.57)**

- **Additional guidelines for secondary schools (2.65)**

    - **Designated grammar schools (2.67)**

    - **Partially selective schools (2.70)**

    - **Partial selection by aptitude (2.72)**

    - **Banding (2.77)**

    - **Requirements as to tests (2.85)**

Fair oversubscription criteria are the key to fair admission arrangements.

2.1   With the exception of designated grammar schools, all maintained schools, including faith schools, that have enough places available **must** offer every child who has applied a place, without condition or the use of any criteria[39]. This includes those schools that use partial selection by ability or aptitude and banding.

2.2   However, many schools will have more applicants than places, and it is essential that the criteria used to allocate places when a school is oversubscribed are fair.

2.3   This chapter provides guidelines on achieving good practice in setting oversubscription criteria for admission authorities to help them ensure that their admission arrangements are fair to all children and their families, and promote social equity rather than working against it. This chapter also prohibits the use of oversubscription criteria that are unfair and **must not** be used (see paragraph 2.13).

2.4   When determining oversubscription criteria all admission authorities **must** ensure that they take account of their statutory responsibilities in respect of children with statements of special educational needs and children in care. Admission authorities **must** ensure that their determined admission arrangements for admissions in September 2008 and subsequent years comply with the mandatory provisions of this Code (see paragraph 2 of the Introduction).

Interviews

2.5   Interviews **must not** be used to determine the extent to which a child meets oversubscription criteria (see paragraphs 1.46 to 1.47).

Children with statements of special educational needs

2.6   All governing bodies are required by section 324 of the Education Act 1996 to admit to the school a child with a statement of special education needs that names the school. This is not an oversubscription criterion. Schools **must** admit such children whether they have places or not.

---

[39] Section 86 of the SSFA 1998.

Children in Care

2.7   Children in care are among the most vulnerable children in society and it is of paramount importance that a school place is found that is in the best interests of the child as quickly as possible. All admission authorities **must** give highest priority in their oversubscription criteria to these children as required by the Education (Admission of Looked after Children) (England) Regulations 2006. The practical effect of this is that in a school's published admission arrangements the first and highest oversubscription criterion **must** be in respect of these children.

Children in Care – faith schools

2.8   The only exception is for faith schools. The admission authorities for these schools may give first priority to all children in care, whether of the faith or not, but **must** give first priority to children in care of their faith above other children of their faith and, where they give any element of priority to children not of their faith, **must** give priority in their oversubscription criteria to looked after children not of their faith above other children not of their faith. More detailed guidelines for faith schools are provided at paragraphs 2.41 to 2.53, and on children in care in Chapter 3.

Achieving good practice in oversubscription criteria

2.9   The most common oversubscription criteria in use are covered in this chapter but it is not possible to create an exhaustive list of what is good practice and what is not. For example, there may be other criteria not mentioned here that are also unfair and therefore **should not** feature in a school's admission arrangements. It is for admission authorities and Admission Forums, acting in accordance with the provisions and guidelines in this Code, to determine which criteria they will use and in what circumstances. In doing so, admission authorities **must** ensure that an effective tie-breaker is included in their arrangements, for example random allocation. Admission Forums **must** encourage all schools in their area to have arrangements that extend choice to parents whatever their social group.

2.10 It is important that parents can easily understand admission arrangements and can assess whether they have a reasonable likelihood of gaining a place at a particular school. Some admission authorities allocate a number of points to particular criteria in order to assess the extent to which oversubscription criteria have been met. Admission authorities **should** avoid using complex points systems that allocate a number of points to different criteria according to their relative importance. If points systems are used they **must** be clear, objective and easily understood.

Parents' right to express a preference

2.11 While they cannot be guaranteed a place at a particular school for their child, parents must be free to express a preference for the school or schools they want for their children. As made clear in Chapter 1, it is important that schools' other policies, for example on school uniform, do not inadvertently discourage applications from poorer families. Oversubscription criteria that amount to the selection of children by schools, by means that disadvantage some social groups compared to others, deny choice to parents and must be eliminated from the system. Paragraph 2.13 accordingly prohibits the use of those criteria that are clearly unfair and can disadvantage some children and families.

2.12 Admission authorities that use criteria that fall within the descriptions in paragraph 2.13 below will be failing in their statutory duty to act in accordance with this Code.

Prohibition of unfair oversubscription criteria

2.13 In setting oversubscription criteria the admission authorities for <u>all</u> maintained schools **must not:**

a) stipulate any conditions that affect the priority given to an application such as taking account of other preferences for schools. For example, by saying that priority will be given if all or some other preferences are for a school with particular characteristics (e.g. other schools are of a particular religious denomination). This includes criteria often described as 'conditionality';

b) give priority to children according to the order of other schools named as preferences by their parents, including 'first preference first' arrangements;

c) give priority to children according to their parents' willingness to give practical support to the ethos of the school or to support the school financially or in some other way;

d) give priority to children according to the occupational, financial or marital status of parents;

e) give priority to children according to the educational achievement or background of their parents;

f) take account of reports from primary or nursery schools about children's past behaviour, attendance, attitude or achievement;

g) discriminate against or disadvantage children with special educational needs or disabilities;

h) allocate places at a school on the basis that a sibling or other relative is a former pupil, including siblings who were on roll at the time of application but will have left by the time the child starts school;

i) take account of the behaviour of other members of a child's family, whether good or bad, including a good or bad attendance record of other children in the same family;

k) give priority to children whose parents are current or former staff or governors or who have another connection to the school, subject to paragraph 2.14 below;

l) give priority to children according to their, or their parents' particular interests, specialist knowledge or hobbies. This does not include taking account of membership of, or participation in, religious activities for faith schools providing this is consistent with this Code and guidance issued by the faith provider body/religious authority;

m) give priority to children based on the order in which applications were received;

n) in the case of designated grammar schools that rank all children according to a pre-determined pass mark and allocate places to those who score highest, give priority to siblings of current or former pupils;

o) in the case of schools with boarding places take account of a child's suitability for boarding (see paragraphs 1.74 to 1.75 and Appendix 6 of this Code).

2.14 The prohibition in 2.13(k) does not prevent an admission authority from offering a place or places to the children of a new appointee to a post at a school after the published offer dates for primary schools, or the national offer date in secondary schools, where there is a demonstrable skills shortage for the vacant post in question, even where this will be in excess of the published admission number, provided that all other relevant law is complied with (see paragraph 1.21). Alternatively, admission authorities may, in these circumstances, place the children of new appointees at the top of any waiting list for places at the school (see paragraph 3.26 to 3.28).

Guidelines on setting fair oversubscription criteria

2.15 This section provides guidelines for, and imposes mandatory requirements on, admission authorities in setting fair oversubscription criteria.

2.16 This Code does not attempt to set out a list of preferred criteria, but rather to discuss each of those commonly used, and the circumstances in which they may be good practice, acceptable or when they are unfair. It is for admission authorities to decide whether any of these criteria are appropriate in their local circumstances, but where they have chosen to depart from the guidance in this Code, admission authorities will have to justify their decision to use the criterion if an objection is made to the Schools Adjudicator.

Siblings of children who are still at the school

2.17 Many parents will want their children to attend the same school and most admission authorities recognise this and give priority in admissions to siblings. This is generally good practice, with the limited exceptions set out below in the case of the small number of partially selective schools which select more than 10% of their intake by aptitude or ability (see paragraph 2.20), and at those designated grammar schools that rank children according to their performance in a test and allocate places to those who score the highest (see paragraph 2.13(n)). Schools that use any form of selection or banding and test children **must** observe the provision at paragraph 2.89. Giving priority to siblings particularly supports families with young children of primary school age who may not be able to travel independently. Admission authorities **should** also consider carefully how other relatives, including those adopted or others living permanently in the household will be treated if a sibling criterion is adopted, and **must** make this clear in information provided to parents including how terms such as step-children will be defined.

Siblings at Primary schools

2.18   Families must be at the heart of the admissions system and the Government expects the admission authorities for primary schools to take the needs of parents with young children into account in deciding which oversubscription criteria will be used. At primary schools it is good practice to give priority to siblings. Admission authorities **should** ensure in their oversubscription criteria that, as far as possible, siblings (including twins, triplets or children from other multiple births) can attend the same primary school, as long as they comply with the infant class size regulations.

Siblings at secondary schools and schools that select 10% or less by ability or aptitude

2.19   At secondary school age, children are usually more independent but many parents will still want their children to attend the same schools. Giving priority to siblings at secondary schools that have no more than 10% selection by ability or aptitude is acceptable and can be good practice.

Siblings at secondary schools that select more than 10% of their intake by ability or aptitude

2.20   A number of secondary schools are permitted under section 100 of the School Standards and Framework Act 1998 to use pre-existing partial selection by ability or aptitude and a number of these admit substantially more than 10% of their intake in this way. Some of these schools give priority for their non-selective places to siblings of children already at the school – whether or not those older siblings secured selective or non-selective places. This reduces the number of non-selective places available to children who do not have siblings at the school. The Government believes that this may lead to the school's intake including a disproportionately high number of children who would have passed the selection test, as some younger siblings would be likely to have passed the selection test if they had taken it. At the same time, the chance for children who would not have passed the test to gain a place at the school would be correspondingly reduced. It is often the case that children admitted by selection are drawn from a much wider area than those who are not and this reduces the number of non-selective places for children who live closer to the school. Where there are a number of partially selective schools in an area this problem is exacerbated.

2.21   The higher the proportion of children admitted by selection at partially selective schools the more likely it is that this will be the case, and the greater the potential for unfairness. Accordingly, the admission authorities for those schools that admit more than 10% of their intake by selection by ability and/or aptitude, if they intend to give priority to siblings, **should** ensure that their admission arrangements as a whole do not exclude families living nearer the school. This might be achieved by using other oversubscription criteria, for example inner and outer catchment areas, where a number of non-selective places are allocated to families living nearer the school while in the outer catchment area priority is given to siblings.

2.22   Where an admission authority for a school that selects more than 10% of its intake by ability and/or aptitude gives priority in its admission arrangements to the siblings of children still at the school they may continue to give priority on the same basis to the younger siblings of pupils who will be on roll at the school before the beginning of the 2008 school year.

2.23   The Adjudicator **must not** uphold an objection that would have the effect of preventing an admission authority from giving priority to children who will have a sibling on roll at the school before the beginning of the 2008 school year in accordance with paragraph 2.22.

Social and medical need

2.24   If admission authorities propose to give higher priority to children for social or medical reasons they **must** ensure that in doing so they are not failing to comply with paragraph 2.13(g) of this Code, which prohibits the use of oversubscription criteria that discriminate against or disadvantage children because of their special educational needs or disabilities.

2.25   Admission authorities **must not** use this criterion to give a child a lower priority in obtaining a place at the school, but it is acceptable to give higher priority to children or families where there is a social or medical need (for example where one or both parents or the child has a disability that may make travel to a school further away more difficult).

2.26   If using this criterion, admission authorities **must** give a clear explanation of what supporting evidence will be required – for example a letter from a registered health professional such as a doctor or social worker – and how this will be assessed objectively. The supporting evidence should set out the particular reasons why the school in question is the most suitable school and the difficulties that would be caused if the child had to attend another school. Admission authorities **must not** give higher priority to children under this criterion if the required documents have not been produced.

2.27   This criterion, if used, **must not** relate to particular aptitudes for some subjects such as in sport or music. For example, schools **must not** seek to admit children, under this criterion, on the basis that they 'need' to attend the school because of an aptitude or interest in sport and the school has particularly good sports facilities. Selection by aptitude is dealt with in paragraphs 2.72 to 2.76 of this Code and schools wishing to admit a proportion of children on the basis of their aptitude for a particular subject **must** follow the guidelines provided there.

Random allocation (lottery)

2.28   Random allocation of school places can be good practice particularly for urban areas and secondary schools. However, it may not be suitable in rural areas. It may be used as the sole means of allocating places or alongside other oversubscription criteria. Random allocation can widen access to schools for those unable to afford to buy houses near to favoured schools and create greater social equity.

2.29   If admission authorities decide to use random allocation when schools are oversubscribed, they need to set out clearly how this will operate, and **must** ensure that arrangements are transparent. They **must** undertake a fresh round of random allocation when deciding which child is to be offered a place from a waiting list, and **must not** use the results of an earlier round of random allocation as this would disadvantage those who had applied for a place at the school after the first random allocation was carried out.

2.30   In order to provide verification that the random allocation process has been carried out fairly, admission authorities **should** ensure that they are supervised by someone independent of the school.

Distance between home and school and ease of access by public transport

2.31   Admission authorities **should** take account of the time it will take to travel to school, and the availability of public transport in establishing their oversubscription criteria.

2.32 Distance between home and school is a clear and objective oversubscription criterion and is often used as a tie breaker in oversubscription criteria. It has the benefit of ensuring that children will not have a disproportionately long journey if access to their nearest school is not possible. Admission authorities **should** explain clearly how distance from home to the school will be measured including the points at the school and the child's home from which distance is to be measured (for example, the main school gate, the front door to the home, how flats will be treated). Admission authorities **must** use a reliable and reasonable system which parents can easily understand. Where a child lives with parents with shared responsibility, each for part of a week, the admission authority **must** make clear how the 'home' address will be determined in a fair and considered way.

2.33 It is good practice to give priority to children who could reach one school (but not others) by public transport, or to children who would have a disproportionately long journey to another school if denied admission to their nearest school.

2.34 As with all oversubscription criteria admission authorities **must** take account of factors that might unfairly advantage or disadvantage one child compared to another. If using distance as a criterion, admission authorities **should** ensure that families who are less able to afford property nearest the school are not excluded.

Catchment areas

2.35 The 1997 Rotherham[40] Judgment confirmed that there is nothing unlawful in the principle of admission authorities operating catchment areas as part of their oversubscription criteria and thereby giving priority to local children whose parents have expressed a preference for the school. However, admission authorities **must not** guarantee places to parents in a local catchment area, in case the pattern of preferences expressed does not allow this guarantee to be met. In drawing up catchment areas, admission authorities **should** ensure that they reflect the diversity of the community served by the school, and **must not** exclude particular housing estates or addresses in a way that might disadvantage particular social groups. A catchment area does not prevent parents expressing a preference for the school if they do not live in the area.

---

[40] R v Rotherham Metropolitan Council ex parte Clark and others [1997] EWCA Civ 2768

2.36   Local authorities and admission authorities **must not** suggest that parents are required to express a preference for the school in whose catchment area they live, or that they have been allocated a place at that school before they have expressed a preference. Local authorities **must** be clear that parents have a statutory right to express a preference for any school they choose, although they **should** explain the possible consequences of not expressing a preference for a school in whose catchment area they live.

2.37   Some schools have adopted inner and outer catchment areas and these work well for some specialist schools in particular by extending choice to more parents. These work by giving priority for a specified number of places in the inner catchment area and the remaining places in the outer area.

2.38   Some schools establish a number of small catchment areas some of which are some distance from school. This practice can exclude some families and if used along with certain other criteria such as partial selection by ability or aptitude or siblings can substantially limit the number of places for families living nearer the school. If using catchment areas in this way admission authorities **should** take into account the possible effect of their other oversubscription criteria and the admission arrangements at other schools in the area in limiting access to the school.

2.39   For children of UK Service personnel and other Crown Servants[41] admission authorities **must** treat a family returning to their area as meeting the residency criteria for that catchment area even if no house is currently owned in that area once proof of the posting has been provided.

2.40   Where catchment areas or distance from the school are used as oversubscription criteria, admission authorities **should** provide a map of the areas, and indicate how far parents within those areas have succeeded in getting places in the past, and whether that is likely to be a guide for the future. Catchment areas **must not** be set after applications have been made.

---

[41] 'A Crown Servant is an officer of the United Kingdom Government. A Crown Servant posted overseas is usually a member of HM forces of a person employed by the Foreign and Commonwealth Office.' (www.hmrc.gov.uk)

Additional guidelines for faith schools

Faith-based oversubscription criteria

2.41 It is unlawful under section 49 of the Equality Act 2006 for maintained, non-maintained or independent schools to discriminate against a child on the grounds of the child's religion or belief in the terms on which it offers to admit him as a pupil or by refusing to accept an application for a place at the school. However, those schools designated by the Secretary of State as having a religious character (faith schools) are exempt and are permitted to use faith-based oversubscription criteria in order to give higher priority in admissions to children who are members of, or who practise, their faith or denomination. This only applies if a school is oversubscribed.

2.42 Faith-based oversubscription criteria **must** be framed so as not to conflict with other legislation, such as equalities and race relations legislation (see Appendix 1) or the mandatory provisions of this Code. As with all other maintained schools, faith schools are required by section 86 of the School Standards and Framework Act 1998 to offer every child who applies, whether of their faith, another faith or no faith, a place at the school if there are places available.

2.43 As with all oversubscription criteria, those that are faith-based must be clear, objective and fair. Parents must easily be able to understand how the criteria will be satisfied. It is primarily for the relevant faith provider group or religious authority to decide how membership or practice is to be demonstrated, and, accordingly, in determining faith-based oversubscription criteria, admission authorities for faith schools **should** only use the methods and definitions agreed by their faith provider group or religious authority (see paragraph 2.47). It is good practice for the governing bodies of all faith schools that are their own admission authority and that are proposing to use faith-based oversubscription criteria to consult their religious authority before going out to statutory consultation with other admission authorities.

2.44 The governing bodies of Church of England schools that are their own admission authorities **must** consult[42] their local Diocesan Board about the admission arrangements they are proposing for their schools before they go out to statutory consultation with other admission authorities, and they **should** follow the Board's advice.

---

[42] Required by section 3(1)(cc) of the Diocesan Boards of Education Measure 1991 (1991 No. 2), as inserted by schedule 13 of Schedule 4 of the 2002 Act

Duty to consult religious authority

2.45   The admission authorities for all faith schools are required to consult such body or person representing their religion or religious denomination as may be prescribed in regulations[43], in addition to consulting other admission authorities, about their admission arrangements. Such religious authorities may refer an objection to the Adjudicator about the arrangements at schools of their faith[44].

2.46   Published admission arrangements **must** make clear how membership or practice is to be demonstrated in line with guidance issued by the faith provider group or religious authority. Whatever method is used it **must** be clearly objective and transparent and therefore any reference requested **must** be in writing and consistent with paragraphs 1.71 to 1.73 of this Code.

Guidance provided by religious authorities

2.47   Religious authorities may provide guidance for the admission authorities of schools of their faith that sets out what objective processes and criteria may be used to establish whether a child is a member of, or whether they practise, the faith. The admission authorities of faith schools that propose to give priority on the basis of membership or practice of their faith **should** have regard to such guidance, to the extent that the guidance is consistent with the mandatory provisions and guidelines of this Code.

2.48   Admission authorities for faith schools **should** consider how their particular admission arrangements impact on the communities in which they are physically based and those faith communities which they serve.

2.49   Where a faith school gives priority for a proportion of places to those of other or no faith in their admission arrangements they **must** be clear how this will work and what oversubscription criteria will be used in their published admission arrangements for each group of places. If the number of applications for one group is less than the number of places available, those places **must** be offered to other children.

---

[43] The Education (Determination of Admission Arrangements) (Amendment) Regulations 1999 (SI 1999/126) as amended by SI 2002/2896 and SI 2007/497

[44] Section 89(2)(e) of the SSFA 1998, as inserted by section 45 of the EIA 2006 and section 90(1) and (11) of the SSFA 1998, as inserted by section 41 of the EIA 2006.

2.50 The governing body of a faith voluntary aided or foundation school which is established after Part 2 of the Education and Inspections Act 2006 comes into force **must** obtain the consent of the appropriate diocesan authority or other body or person representing the religion or religious denomination as may be prescribed under section 89(2)(e) for consultative purposes, before proposing or determining admission arrangements which give priority for a proportion of places to children otherwise than on the basis of whether that child is a member of or practises the relevant religion or religious denomination.

2.51 The mandatory requirement in paragraph 2.50 does not apply in the case of children in care. Paragraphs 2.7 and 2.8 provide detailed guidelines on children in care[45].

2.52 The Adjudicator in considering any objections to the admission arrangements of schools described in 2.50 above **must not** uphold any objection that would have the effect of giving priority for a proportion of places to children other than on the basis of whether that child is a member of or practises the relevant religion or religious denomination without the consent referred to in that paragraph.

2.53 The Adjudicator in considering any objections to the admission arrangements of any voluntary aided or foundation schools with a religious character (regardless of when the school was established) **must** uphold an objection where the statutory requirement in respect of children in care has not been complied with.

Additional guidelines for boarding schools

2.54 Boarding schools have an important role in providing places for the most vulnerable children and in providing a stable educational environment for those who need it, including those whose parents have jobs or careers which dictate that they often have to work outside the country. Boarding schools **must** therefore, after giving the required priority to children in care, give next highest priority in their oversubscription criteria for boarding places to children with a 'boarding need'. Boarding schools **must** ensure that it is clear to parents what is meant by 'boarding need' in their published admission arrangements.

---

[45] The Education (Admission of Looked After Children) (England) Regulations 2006 (SI 2006/128).

Boarding need

2.55 Children with a boarding need include:

a) children at risk or with an unstable home environment;

b) children of members of the British forces overseas and of other key workers and Crown Servants working abroad (e.g. the children of charity workers, people working for voluntary service organisations, the diplomatic service or the European Union, teachers, law enforcement officers and medical staff working abroad) whose work dictates that they spend much of the year overseas.

Additional guidelines for primary schools

2.56 The law does not require a child to start school until the start of the term following the child's fifth birthday. The date compulsory school age is reached is determined by dates set by the Secretary of State for the autumn, spring and summer terms. These are 31 August, 31 December and 31 March. Academic selection **must not** be used to decide entry into primary education.

Infant classes

2.57 Infant classes[46] (i.e. those where the majority of children will reach the age of 5, 6, or 7 during the school year) **must not** contain more than 30 pupils[47] with a single school teacher[48]. While admission can be refused on normal prejudice grounds once an admission number of lower than 30 (or multiples of 30) has been reached, admissions **must** be refused on "infant class-size prejudice" grounds where the published admission number allows for classes of 30, and the school would have to take 'qualifying' measures to keep to the statutory class size limit if more children were admitted e.g. employ another teacher.

2.58 The class size legislation makes allowance for the entry of an additional child in very limited circumstances where not to admit the child would be prejudicial to his or her interests ('excepted pupils'). However, every effort **must** be made to keep over large classes to a minimum. These circumstances are where:

---

[46] Further information can be found at www.teachernet.gov.uk/educationoverview/briefing/currentstrategy/infantclasssizes/

[47] The Education (Infant Class Sizes) (England) Regulations 1998 (SI 1998 /1973) as amended by SI 2006/3409

[48] A person who is qualified under the Education (School Teachers' Qualifications) (England) Regulations 2003 (SI 2003/1662).

a) a child moves into an area outside the normal admissions round and no other school would provide suitable education (i.e. provide access to the National Curriculum) within a reasonable distance of their home. Before admitting children under this exception, admission authorities **must** consult their local authority who are in a position to advise whether these conditions apply;

b) the school is named on a child's statement of special educational needs, when that child has either been assessed or moved into the area outside the normal admissions round;

c) a child in care is admitted outside the normal admissions round;

d) a child wins an appeal having initially been refused entry as a result of an error in implementing the school's admission arrangements, or because the decision to refuse admission was not one which a reasonable admission authority would have made in the circumstances of the case;

e) a child normally educated in a special school or special educational needs unit attached to a mainstream school attends an infant class in the mainstream school, where this has been deemed as beneficial to the child. This also applies to those children registered both at special and mainstream schools.

2.59 In the first four of these cases, the class may only be above 30 for that school year or the remainder of that school year. Qualifying measures must be taken for the following year, or the class will be unlawfully large.

Admission of children below compulsory school age

2.60 When determining the arrangements for primary schools that admit children below compulsory school age, the admission authority **must** make it clear that:

a) the arrangements do not apply to those being admitted for nursery education including nursery provision delivered in a co-located children's centre;

b) parents of children who are admitted for nursery education will still need to apply for a place at the school if they want their child to transfer to the reception class;

c) attendance at the nursery or co-located children's centre does not guarantee admission to the school; and

d) parents can request that the date their child is admitted to the school is deferred until later in the school year or until the child reaches compulsory school age in that school year.

Primary schools with attached nursery class

2.61 Where schools have a nursery class attached, separate admission arrangements **must** be published for entry to the nursery. Published admission arrangements **must** make clear to parents that attendance in the nursery class does not guarantee admission to the school for primary education, and that a separate application must be made for transfer from nursery to primary school (as it must for transfers from infant to junior schools).

Giving priority to children attending the school's nursery or co-located children's centre

2.62 Admission authorities that propose to give priority to children who attend the nursery or the co-located children's centre for nursery education **should** ensure that families that live nearer the school, those who choose to take up other nursery options or the free entitlement at an alternative local provider, or those who have recently moved to the area, are not disadvantaged compared to other families.

2.63 Admission authorities **should** take into account the totality of provision for three and four year olds in their relevant area when making changes to arrangements for admission to full time education. Three year old children **should not** normally be admitted to reception classes, except where, in exceptional circumstances and as part of development of a local authority supported Foundation Stage Unit or Sure Start Children's Centre on site, there may be good reason to combine nursery and reception classes. If a school wishes to alter its age range to admit a younger age group, it will need to publish statutory proposals.

Deferred entry to primary schools

2.64   Where admission authorities for primary schools offer places in reception classes to parents before their children are of compulsory school age, they **should** offer the parents the option of deferring their child's entry until later in the same school year. The effect is that the place is held for that child and is not available to be offered to another child. The parent would not however be able to defer entry beyond the beginning of the term after the child's fifth birthday, nor beyond the academic year for which the original application was accepted. If they want to defer their child's admission to a later academic year, they will have to reapply during the appropriate admissions round. This **must** be made clear in the admission arrangements for the school.

Additional guidelines for secondary schools

Selection by ability

2.65   Section 39 of the Education and Inspections Act 2006, which re-states section 99 of the School Standards and Framework Act 1998 , prohibits the introduction of any new selection by ability, other than for banding (see paragraphs 2.77 to 2.84) or for sixth forms.

Feeder primary schools

2.66   The use of named feeder schools allows local continuity and can support good curriculum and geographical links between phases in an area. Admission authorities **must** ensure that such arrangements do not disadvantage children from more deprived areas, for example they **must not** include only feeder primaries that serve more advantaged groups and leave out schools that are a similar distance from the school but serve less advantaged groups.

Designated grammar schools

2.67   Like all other maintained schools, the admission authorities for designated grammar schools are required to act in accordance with this code. Grammar schools are permitted to select children on the basis of high academic ability, and to leave places unfilled if they have insufficient applicants of the required standard. Most assess ability by means of a test, but they may apply any fair and objective means of assessing ability they consider appropriate. Admission authorities **must** ensure that parents are aware that meeting the academic requirements for entry to a grammar school is not, in itself, a guarantee of a grammar school place.

2.68 Methods of allocating places for oversubscribed grammar schools vary. Some admission authorities allocate available places in rank order of performance in the entrance test; admission authorities for these schools **must not** give priority to siblings (see paragraph 2.13(n)). Others set a pass mark and then apply other oversubscription criteria to determine which of the candidates who have passed will be offered a place; admission authorities for these schools may use any permitted oversubscription criteria. Grammar schools **must not** use oversubscription criteria prohibited by this Code.

2.69 Some admission authorities for grammar schools use a review system to consider whether children who have marginally failed to reach the required standard in the entrance test could be deemed as being of grammar school ability. This is not a statutory process, and does not replace a parent's formal right of appeal against refusal of a place. In view of the need to co-ordinate allocation of places such reviews **must** be completed before places are allocated, so that children who are deemed as being of grammar school ability as a result of the review can be considered for allocation of places at the same time as others.

Partially selective schools

2.70 Whereas grammar schools are wholly selective by academic ability, partially selective schools select just a proportion of their pupil intake by ability or by aptitude, and partial selection is effectively an oversubscription criterion. If there are insufficient children who have satisfied the published entry requirements for a selective place the places **must** be offered to other children. Partially selective schools **must not** keep places unfilled if they have applications for them. For the purposes of the legislation on selection, schools which call themselves "bilateral schools", because they admit some children on the basis of ability and operate a "grammar" stream alongside a "comprehensive" stream, are considered to be partially selective schools.

2.71 The School Standards and Framework Act 1998 and supporting regulations allow the following forms of partial selection:

a) priority for up to 10% of pupils on the basis of aptitude[49] in certain subjects in limited circumstances and where the school has a specialism; however, new selection in design and technology and ICT is prohibited from entry in 2008/09 (see paragraph 2.74);

---

[49] Aptitude tests must test for the subject aptitude concerned and not test for ability or any other aptitude.

b) partial selection by ability or aptitude that existed at the beginning of the 1997/98 school year and which could not now be lawfully introduced (pre-existing partial selection). Admission authorities may continue to use this form of selection but only if the proportion of children selected does not exceed the lowest proportion at any time since the beginning of the 1997/98 school year and the basis for selection has remained unchanged[50].

Partial selection by aptitude

2.72 Selection by aptitude in sport and PE, the visual and performing arts and modern foreign languages can play an important part in widening access to particular schools. Section 102 of the 1998 Act allows the admission authority for a school with a specialism in one or more prescribed subjects to give priority to up to 10% of children who can demonstrate an aptitude in the relevant subject. This flexibility is not restricted to schools in the specialist schools programme, but does require that the school has a particular expertise or facility.

2.73 Giving priority for places by aptitude is, in effect, an oversubscription criterion and an admission authority **must not** leave places unfilled if there are not enough children to fill the proportion of selective aptitude places. In this case those places **must** be filled by children using the school's published non-selective oversubscription criteria.

2.74 The relevant subjects[51] are:

a) physical education or sport, or one or more sports;

b) the performing arts, or any one or more of those arts;

c) the visual arts, or any one or more of those arts;

d) modern foreign languages, or any such language;

e) design and technology, and ICT. Schools already selecting in those subjects before the 2008 school year may continue to do so, but no further selection in these subjects can be introduced in respect of subsequent years.

---

[50] Section 100 of SSFA 1998 as amended by section 53 of EIA 2006

[51] The Education (Aptitude for Particular Subjects) Regulations 1999 as amended by SI 2006/3408

2.75 A child with aptitude is one who is identified as being able to benefit from teaching in a specific subject, or who demonstrates a particular capacity to succeed in that subject. When considering whether the child has an aptitude for a subject the admission authority **must** determine whether a child demonstrates a particular capacity to learn or to develop skills in that subject, and that he or she can benefit from the particular expertise and facilities at that school.

2.76 The 10% limit is an overall limit, regardless of the number of subjects in which the school specialises. This means that if a school specialises in, for example, the visual arts and sport, 5% of places might be allocated to children who demonstrate an aptitude in the visual arts and 5% to those who demonstrate an aptitude in sport. The proportion allocated in each subject is up to the admission authority to decide, but the total of places allocated on the grounds of aptitude **must not** amount to more than 10%[52].

Banding

2.77 Banding, like other oversubscription criteria, only operates when the number of applications exceeds the number of places. Schools which use banding **must not** apply another test of ability once applicants are allocated to bands; they **must not** give priority within bands according to performance in the test. The admission authority **must** apply its other oversubscription criteria (such as random allocation) to each band to allocate places.

2.78 Banding is permitted by section 101 of the School Standards and Framework Act 1998, as amended by section 54 of the Education and Inspections Act 2006. The Education and Inspections Act 2006 removed the need for approval of statutory proposals before the introduction of banding arrangements, and this can now be done as part of the annual admissions consultation process.

2.79 Pupil ability banding is used by some admission authorities to ensure that their intake includes a proportionate spread of children of different abilities. Banding arrangements are good practice, provided the arrangements are fair, objective and not used as a means of unlawfully admitting a disproportionate number of high ability children.

---

[52] The Education (Proportion of Selective Admissions) Regulations 1998 (SI 1998 / 2229)

2.80 Banding may be adopted in relation to individual schools, two or more schools operating together, or across a local authority area. Banding arrangements which are already in place may continue unchanged but the admission authorities for a school or groups of schools working together may now adopt admission arrangements that band applicants to produce an intake that is representative of:

a) the full range of ability of applicants for the school(s); or

b) the range of ability of children in the local area; or

c) the national ability range.

2.81 If places become vacant in some bands, for example, because parents accept offers of places at other schools, and no applicants in those bands remain without a place, they **should** be evenly filled by children falling into the next nearest bands (i.e. the bands on either side, or below or above, if the first child is from the band above then the next **should** be from the one below).

Banding that existed prior to the School Standards and Framework Act 1998

2.82 Banding which it would not be possible to introduce now - for example, because the effect is to favour high ability children disproportionately - but which was in place at the beginning of the 1997/98 school year and continuously since then on the same basis, may continue. This is allowed as a form of pre-existing partial selection and any admission authorities with such arrangements are required to publish a notice explaining their arrangements in a local newspaper, giving parents the opportunity to object to the Adjudicator about the arrangements.

Partial selection by aptitude and banding

2.83 Section 101(5) of the School Standards and Framework Act 1998 allows admission authorities which use banding also to admit up to 10% of children in total on the basis of aptitude for one or more of the prescribed subjects. So, for example, admission authorities are able to admit the first 10% of children on the basis of aptitude and band the remaining 90%, or band children first and then admit 10% of each band on the basis of the relevant aptitude.

Children with special educational needs and banding

2.84 Children with special educational needs can be included in banding arrangements, that is they can be allocated to the band appropriate to their ability, but schools **must not** refuse to admit a child with a statement that names the school.

Requirements as to tests

Test arrangements for banding and partial selection by aptitude

2.85   It is up to the admission authority to decide which tests will be used to determine the band in which to place an individual child, but it **must** ensure that any test arrangements (including the reasons for testing) are explained clearly to parents and that adequate notice is given on the location and length of tests. Where a number of schools in an area band, they **should** use a common test, such as the results of QCA Year 5 optional tests conducted in primary schools, to ensure that children are not required to take more than one test.

2.86   Whatever form of test is used to band, it **must** be designed to give an accurate reflection of the abilities of all children irrespective of sex, race or disability.

2.87   Tests, assessments or auditions used to identify whether a child has an aptitude for a particular subject **must** be objective, have a distinctive subject focus and **must not** discriminate against applicants on the grounds of sex, race, disability or family background. And the assessment **must** test only for the subject aptitude concerned and not for ability or any other aptitude or for prior learning or experience in the subject. If there are two or more schools using tests in an area the same aptitude test **should** be used.

General provisions relating to all tests

2.88   Tests **should** be at times likely to be convenient to parents with varying working patterns.

2.89   Admission authorities **must not** adjust the score achieved by any child in a test in order to take account of oversubscription criteria, such as having a sibling at the school.

2.90   It is unlawful to charge a fee for, or in connection with, admission to any maintained school. This includes fees designed to cover the administrative costs of selection and testing arrangements, even if these are refundable to successful candidates. Inviting parents to give voluntary financial support to the school, however conditional, before admission decisions are taken could be seen as a disguised fee and is unlawful.

2.91   Admission authorities **must** ensure that tests are accessible to children with special educational needs and disabilities. For example, it may be appropriate to make available test material in an adapted format, or allow additional time, or a scribe, depending on the individual needs of the child.

Information for parents – outcome of entry tests

2.92 Grammar schools and other schools, or their admission authorities, which are permitted to use selection by ability or aptitude, **should** ensure that parents are informed of the outcome of entry tests before they make their applications for other schools.

Chapter 3

Admission Arrangements In-Year and Outside the Normal Admissions Round and Fair Access Protocols

This chapter provides guidelines on, and where appropriate imposes mandatory requirements on, applications for school places outside the normal admissions round, in particular on

- **Establishing arrangements for children who arrive in the area outside the normal admissions round (3.1)**

- **Information sharing when a child moves school (3.4)**

- **Direction of admission of children in care (3.7)**

- **Children who have been permanently excluded twice (3.10)**

- **Children with challenging behaviour (3.11)**

- **In-year fair access protocols (3.14)**

- **Admission of children of UK service personnel and other Crown servants, including diplomats (3.22)**

- **Waiting lists (3.26)**

Applications for school places outside the normal admissions round

3.1   In dealing with applications for school places outside the normal admissions round, whether in-year or at the start of a school year which is not a normal point of entry to the school, admission authorities **must** comply with parental preference unless one of the statutory reasons for refusing admission applies. Such applications **must** be considered without delay, and a formal decision either to offer or to refuse a place **must** be made and notified to the applicant, advising them of their statutory right of appeal when a place cannot be offered. Applicants **must not** be refused the opportunity to make an application, or told that they can only be placed on a waiting list rather than make a formal application.

3.2   The same statutory reasons for refusing admission apply outside the normal admission round as with applications made during the normal admissions round. The following list is not exhaustive. Admission authorities **must not** refuse to admit a child solely because:

a)   They have applied later than other applicants;

b)   They are not of the faith of the school in the case of a faith school;

c)   They followed a different curriculum at their previous school;

d)   Information has not been received from their previous school;

e)   They have missed entrance tests for selective places. In these circumstances the admission authority has a number of options. It can arrange for an entrance test to be conducted; seek other evidence of the child's academic ability; or (if the school has no places available) refuse admission on the basis that admission of an additional child would cause prejudice to the 'efficient provision of education or efficient use of resources', in which case an appeal panel would have to consider an appeal on the working assumption that the child was of the required academic standard.

3.3   In establishing co-ordinated admission schemes local authorities **must** set out how late applications and arrangements for admissions outside the normal admission round will be handled. The admissions process **must** be co-ordinated beyond the offer date, at least until late applicants have been offered schools and places which become available because of rejected offers, for example, have been reallocated. Local authorities and Admission Forums **must** also consider how the admissions process in-year and for years which are not a normal point of entry to schools could be better co-ordinated so that local authorities can track movement of individual children into and around their area, and so that children spend only the minimum possible time out of school.

Information sharing when a child moves school

3.4   When a child moves from one school to another in England (either maintained or independent), the governing body of the school that the child moves from **must** transfer their educational record to the new school no later than 15 school days after the child ceases to be registered there. Where the governing body of the school does not know which school the child has transferred to, and it is not reasonably practicable for it to find out (e.g. by telephoning or writing to the parents), it **should** send a common transfer file for that pupil via the Secure Data Transfer (S2S) website[53] identifying the destination school as 'unknown'. This information is then stored in the Lost Pupil Database. Schools which do not receive common transfer files for new pupils can ask local authority contacts to search this database to see if the files are there.

3.5   Admission authorities **must not** adopt procedures or criteria that disadvantage children who arrive in their relevant area outside the normal admission round. And arrangements **must** be in place for Gypsy, Roma and Traveller children to be quickly registered at a school whether they are residing permanently or temporarily in the area.

Children in Care

3.6   Regulations[54] made under the School Standards and Framework Act 1998 require admission authorities to give children in care highest priority in their admission arrangements, and this will ensure that they are guaranteed admission to preferred schools at normal time of entry (see paragraphs 2.7 and 2.8).

Power to direct admission of Children in Care

3.7   Outside the normal admissions round, local authorities may direct other admission authorities for any maintained school to admit a child in their care to the school best suited to his or her needs[55]. Such action **must** be taken in the best interests of the child. Before giving a direction the local authority **must** consult the admission authority for the school they propose to specify in the direction. The admission authority then has seven days to inform the local authority if it is willing to admit the child without being directed to do so.

---

[53] www.teachernet.gov.uk/S2S

[54] The Education (Admission of Looked After Children) (England) Regulations 2006(SI 2006/128).

[55] Section 97A to 97C of the SSFA 1998 as inserted by section 50 of the EIA 2006.

3.8   If, following the consultation, the local authority decides to issue the direction it **must** first inform the admission authority, the governing body (if the governing body is not the admission authority), the head teacher and, if the school is in another local authority area, the maintaining local authority. If the admission authority (or the governing body if it is not the admission authority and only in relation to a child in care who has previously been excluded from at least two schools) considers that admission of the child would seriously prejudice the provision of efficient education or efficient use of resources, the admission authority has seven days in which to refer the case to the Adjudicator. The Adjudicator may either uphold the direction, or, if the local authority that looks after the child agrees, determine that another school in England **must** admit the child. The Adjudicator's decision is binding. The Adjudicator may not direct an alternative school to admit a child when the child has already been excluded from that school or when admission would seriously prejudice the provision of efficient education or efficient use of resources.

3.9   Where local authorities believe that a particular Academy will best meet the needs of the child, they can ask them to admit that child even when the Academy is full. A consensus will be reached locally in the large majority of cases, but if the Academy disagrees with the local authority's reasoning and refuses to admit the child, the case can be referred to the Secretary of State. In such cases, the Secretary of State may direct an Academy to admit a child in care, and can seek advice from the Adjudicator in reaching his decision[56]. In providing such advice, the Adjudicator will consider the case in the same way as for maintained schools.

---

[56] Section 25(3A) of the SSFA 1998 (as inserted by section 163 of the EIA 2006)

Children who have been permanently excluded twice

3.10 Where their child has been permanently excluded from two or more schools, a parent can still express a preference for a school place, but the requirement to comply with that preference is removed for a period of two years from the date on which the latest exclusion took place[57]. This does not apply to: children with statements of special educational needs; children who were below compulsory school age when excluded; children who were reinstated following a permanent exclusion; and children who would have been reinstated following a permanent exclusion had it been practicable to do so. A permanent exclusion is regarded as taking effect from the first school day the head teacher has told the child not to attend school. The admission authority for the school may refuse to admit a child who has been excluded twice, or in the case of a community or voluntary controlled school, the governing body may appeal against the decision of the local authority as the admission authority to admit the child (see the School Admission Appeals Code for information on these appeals). Local authorities are still responsible for providing suitable full-time education for these children and may need to use their powers of direction or provide a place in a Pupil Referral Unit.

Children with challenging behaviour

3.11 Admission authorities **must not** refuse to admit children in or outside the normal admission round on the basis of their behaviour elsewhere, unless paragraph 3.10 applies. They also **must not** refuse to admit a child thought to be potentially disruptive, or to exhibit challenging behaviour, on the grounds that the child is to first be assessed for special educational needs. The law disapplies the normal principle that parents' preferences are complied with only in the 'twice excluded' situation described in paragraph 3.10. If, following admission, a child is found to be seriously and persistently disruptive, the school may consider disciplinary action in the normal way, including temporary and, ultimately, permanent exclusion procedures. A child with challenging behaviour may also be disabled as defined in the Disability Discrimination Act 1995 and require reasonable adjustments to be made for them in the school or require particular support for any special educational needs.

---

[57] Section 87 of the SSFA 1998.

3.12   Some undersubscribed schools may find that they have been required to admit an undue proportion of children with a recent history of challenging behaviour, which may have led to a permanent exclusion from another school. Implementation of an In-Year Fair Access Protocol will result in all schools admitting a more even share of such children, including children excluded from other schools.

3.13   Exceptionally, outside the normal year of entry, and where an application is made outside arrangements covered by an In-Year Fair Access Protocol, admission authorities may decide to refuse to admit a child with challenging behaviour even though there are places available, on the grounds that admission would prejudice the provision of efficient education or the efficient use of resources. This will normally only be appropriate where a school has a particularly high concentration of children with challenging behaviour or previously excluded children and one or more of the following exceptional circumstances exists, namely that the school:

a) requires special measures or has recently come out of them (within the last two years);

b) has been identified by Ofsted as having serious weaknesses or requiring significant improvement and therefore given 'notice to improve';

c) is subject to a formal warning notice;

d) is a Fresh Start school or Academy open for less than two years; or

e) is a secondary school where less than 30% of children are achieving 5 or more GCSEs at grades A*–C, or a primary school where fewer than 65% of pupils achieve level 4 of above at Key Stage 2 in both English and mathematics for four or more consecutive years.

In-Year Fair Access Protocols

3.14   In-Year Fair Access Protocols (formerly referred to as 'hard to place pupil protocols') exist to ensure that access to education is secured quickly for children who have no school place, and to ensure that all schools in an area admit their fair share of children with challenging behaviour. Along with devolved funding and responsibility for alternative provision, an agreed protocol encourages schools to work together in partnership to improve behaviour and tackle persistent absence.

3.15 All admission authorities and Admission Forums **must** have Fair Access Protocols in place by September 2007. In addition, all schools and Academies **must** participate in their local authority area's protocol in order to ensure that unplaced children, especially the most vulnerable, are offered a place at a suitable school as quickly as possible. This includes admitting children above the published admission number to schools that are already full. For that reason, admission appeal panels **should not** view the fact that a protocol has obliged a school to admit over its admission number as an indication that it can do so in the normal admissions round without causing prejudice to the efficient provision of education or efficient use of resources.

3.16 There is a balance to be struck between finding a place quickly, when the place might be in an undersubscribed school or one facing challenging circumstances, and finding a school place that is appropriate for the child. In agreeing a protocol the local authority, Admission Forums and admission authorities **should** ensure that no school, including those with places available, is asked to take an excessive or unreasonable number of children who have been excluded from other schools.

3.17 Admission authorities and Admission Forums **must** ensure that all children who arrive outside the normal admissions round who may have difficulty securing a place are covered in their protocol. Children with special educational needs but without statements **should** be treated in the same way as all other applicants, but protocols **must** include arrangements for ensuring that, where there is prior need for particular support or for reasonable adjustments to be made for children with special educational needs or disabilities, such children are placed quickly. Children with statements of special educational needs that name a school and who arrive outside the normal admission round **must** be admitted to the school even if the school is full. Similarly, where a local authority, as the corporate parent, directs an admission authority to admit a child in care, the governing body **must** admit the child to the school at any specified time during the year, even if the school is full, unless the Adjudicator upholds an appeal from the admission authority[58].

---

[58] Section 97(3) of the SSFA 1998 as amended by section 49 of the EIA 2006

3.18 The governing body of a voluntary aided or foundation school may under section 97 of the School Standards and Framework Act 1998 (as amended by section 49 of the Education and Inspections Act 2006) refer a local authority's decision to direct the admission of a child in accordance with a locally agreed protocol under section 96 of the School Standards and Framework Act 1998 to the Schools Adjudicator. The Adjudicator then determines which school is to be required to admit the child. The governing body of the school **must** admit the child. If a governing body refuses to comply with a direction under section 96 the local authority may refer the matter to the Secretary of State for consideration under section 497 of the Education Act 1996. Similarly, the local authority can refer the matter to the Secretary of State if an Academy refuses to admit a child in accordance with a protocol. In the case of a community or voluntary controlled school where the governing body refuses to accept the local authority decision as admission authority to admit the child, the local authority may refer the matter to the Secretary of State under section 496 or section 497 of the Education Act 1996.

3.19 Once In-Year Fair Access protocols have been agreed Admission Forums **must** monitor how well they are working[59], how quickly the children are found places, and the contribution every school in the area is making. Additional guidance, along with example protocols and case studies of good practice can be found at www.dfes.gov.uk/sacode.

---

[59] The Education (Admissions Forums)(England) Regulations 2002 (SI 2002/2900) as amended by SI 2007/192

Local authority powers to direct admission to a foundation or voluntary aided school

3.20 Local authorities have important powers to direct the governing body of a school that is the admission authority to admit a child, where they have been refused admission to, or permanently excluded[60] from, every school which is both a reasonable distance from their home and provides suitable education. This is provided that the school which the local authority directs is a reasonable distance from the child's home and not one from which he/she has been permanently excluded[61]. The governing body of the school, which the local authority has notified of its intention to direct, may, within 15 days of receiving notice to that effect, refer the matter to the Schools Adjudicator for determination. A local authority may not make a direction under this provision where the admission of the child concerned would result in class size-related 'prejudice'. As with children in care, local authorities can ask Academies to admit a child in the same circumstances. Where an Academy refuses to admit the child, the local authority can refer the matter to the Secretary of State for consideration of whether or not to direct the Academy to admit the child.

Local authority decisions to admit a child to a community or voluntary controlled school

3.21 Governing bodies of community and voluntary controlled schools **must** implement any decision made by the local authority relating to admission of children[62], except where this relates to the admission of a child who has been permanently excluded twice (see paragraph 3.10).

Admission of children of UK Service personnel and other Crown servants (including Diplomats) outside the normal admissions round

3.22 Families of UK Service personnel and other Crown servants are subject to frequent movement within the UK and from abroad, often at relatively short notice. School places **should** be allocated to children and their families in advance of the approaching school year if accompanied by an official MOD, FCO or GCHQ letter declaring a relocation date, and admission authorities **should** consider notifying results of applications electronically, where this is acceptable to the applicant, especially where families are still abroad.

---

[60] Section 96 of the SSFA 1998
[61] Section 96 of the SSFA 1998 as amended by Schedule 4 to the EA 2002
[62] Section 88(1A) of the SSFA 1998, as inserted by section 43 of the EIA 2006

3.23 Local authorities and admission authorities **must**:

a) ensure that the needs of the children of these families are taken into account;

b) allocate a school place in advance, if the applicant would meet the criteria when they are relocated;

c) invite a Service representative or representatives of other Crown servants (e.g. GCHQ personnel) to join the Admission Forum where there are significant concentrations of such personnel in an area; and

d) accept a Unit postal address for applications from service personnel in the absence of a new home postal address.

3.24 Admission authorities **must not**:

a) reserve places for blocks of these children; or

b) refuse a place to such a child because the family does not currently live in the local authority area.

Timing of admission

3.25 While it is essential that children who have no school place are found one quickly, section 433 of the Education Act 1996 permits deferment of admission to the start of a school term. In cases involving school transfers that do not require a house move, or where there is no need for an immediate move, admission authorities may wish to arrange for a child to join them at the beginning of term to minimise disruption to their own and other children's education.

Waiting lists

3.26 Admission authorities are not required to maintain waiting lists for oversubscribed schools but where they intend to do so, they **must** include this information in their school's published admission arrangements, making clear that children will be ranked in the same order as the published oversubscription criteria. Waiting lists **must** be clear, fair and objective and **must not** give priority to children based on the date either their application was received or their name was added to the list. For example, if a child moves to an area outside the normal admissions round and has higher priority against the published oversubscription criteria, they **must** be ranked above those with lower priority already on the list. Admission authorities **must** notify parents of where their child has been placed on a waiting list but **must not** give any indication of the likelihood of being offered a place as their position may change.

3.27 As soon as school places become vacant, admission authorities **must** fill these vacancies from any waiting list, even if this is before admission appeals have been heard. Placing a child's name on a waiting list does not affect a parent's right of appeal against an unsuccessful application.

3.28 Children who are the subject of a direction by a local authority to admit or who are allocated to a school in accordance with an In-Year Fair Access Protocol, **must** take precedence over those on a waiting list (see paragraphs 3.14 to 3.19). Where an admission authority holds a waiting list, they **must** make clear in their admission arrangements that these children will take precedence over any child already on that list. Legislation enables this to be done immediately without the need to apply to the Schools Adjudicator for a variation in determined admission arrangements[63].

---

[63] The School Admissions (Alteration and Variation of, and Objections to, Arrangements) (England) Regulations 2007 (SI 2007/496)

Chapter 4

Ensuring a Fair Admissions System

This chapter provides guidelines on monitoring and enforcing this Code to ensure a fair admissions system.

Ensuring a fair admissions system is the responsibility of all those who have a duty to act in accordance with the Code.

4.1   This Code has so far described the importance of ensuring clear, objective and fair admission arrangements that are easily understood and that are robust enough to ensure that all children have an equal opportunity to achieve their full potential and to enjoy their time at school. If these aims are to be achieved, it is important that the mandatory requirements imposed by the law and by this Code are complied with and the guidelines it provides are followed.

4.2 This chapter sets out the important role that local authorities, Admission Forums and the Schools Adjudicator have in ensuring that all school admission arrangements are fair and comply with admission law and the requirements of this Code. It also describes the new right of parents to refer objections to the Schools Adjudicator if they consider that admission arrangements are unlawful or do not comply with the mandatory requirements of this Code. This will ensure that admission arrangements serve the interests of all families in local communities.

Admission Authorities

4.3 All school admission authorities **must** ensure that the determined admission arrangements for which they are responsible, comply with admissions law and are in accordance with the provisions of this Code. Governing bodies that are their own admission authorities are encouraged to ensure that they are represented on the Admission Forum for their area, as this gives them the opportunity to contribute to ensuring a fair admissions system. Admission authorities **should** use their power to refer an objection to the Schools Adjudicator if the admission arrangements at schools contravene admissions law, do not comply with the mandatory provisions of this Code or fail to follow its guidelines without justification.

Local Authorities

4.4 Local authorities have a duty under section 13A of the Education Act 1996 (as substituted by the Education and Inspections Act 2006) to ensure fair access to educational opportunity and have a key role in ensuring that school admission arrangements are lawful and comply with the mandatory provisions of this Code. They **must** ensure that admission arrangements for schools in their area for which they are the admission authority are clear, objective and fair.

4.5 In order for parents to exercise their right to object (see paragraph 4.14), local authorities **must** publish a notice in a local newspaper as soon as all the admission arrangements for schools in their area have been determined, setting out that details of these are available for inspection at the local authority's offices and such other places as the local authority may decide[64].

---

[64] The Education (Determination of Admission Arrangements) (Amendment) Regulations 1999 (SI 1999/126) as amended by SI 2002/2896 and SI 2007/497

Requirement on local authorities to object to unfair admission arrangements

4.6   Local authorities **must** use their powers to refer objections to the Schools Adjudicator if they consider, or are made aware of, any admission arrangements proposed by any other admission authority that are unlawful, that do not comply with the mandatory requirements or guidelines in this Code, or that appear to be unfair, unclear, subjective or encouraging social segregation.

4.7   Local authorities **must** also consider carefully any representations they receive from parents about the admission arrangements for schools for which they are not the admission authority and whether they will use their power to make an objection to the Adjudicator.

4.8   Local authorities may be held to account by the Local Government Ombudsman if, having been made aware admission arrangements that are unfair, unlawful or do not comply with this Code, they do not refer objections to the Schools Adjudicator.

Admission Forums

4.9   Section 85A of the School Standards and Framework Act 1998 requires all local authorities to establish an Admission Forum[65]. Admission Forums provide a vehicle for admission authorities and other key interested parties to discuss the effectiveness of local admission arrangements, consider how to deal with difficult admission issues and advise admission authorities on ways in which their arrangements can be improved. Admission authorities of all maintained schools and Academies, when exercising their functions, **must** have regard to any advice offered by the Forum. Local authorities may establish a joint forum with one or more other local authorities to consider and advise on admissions in more than one authority area. Further information on the membership and procedures of Admission Forums is set out in Appendix 2.

Statutory role of Admission Forums

4.10 Admission Forums have a key role in ensuring a fair admissions system that promotes social equity and **must**, under section 84 of the School Standards and Framework Act 1998, act in accordance with this Code. The role of Admission Forums is set out in Regulations[66]. Admission Forums **must**:

---

[65] The Education (Admission Forums) (England) Regulations 2002 (SI 2002/2900) as amended by SI 2007/192

[66] Education (Admission Forums) (England) Regulations 2002 (SI 2002/2900) as amended by SI 2007/192

a) consider how well existing and proposed admission arrangements serve the interests of children and parents within the area of the authority;

b) promote agreement on admission issues;

c) consider the comprehensiveness and accessibility of the admissions literature and information produced for parents by each admission authority within the area of the forum;

d) consider the effectiveness of the authority's proposed co-ordinated admission arrangements;

e) consider the means by which admissions processes might be improved and how actual admissions relate to the admission numbers published;

f) monitor the admission of children who arrive in the authority's area outside a normal admission round with a view to promoting arrangements for the fair distribution of such children among local schools, taking account of any preference expressed in accordance with arrangements made under section 86(1) of the School Standards and Framework Act 1998 and in accordance with this Code (see Chapter 3);

g) promote the arrangements for children with special educational needs, children in care and children who have been excluded from school;

h) consider any other admissions issues that arise.

Ensuring fair access

4.11 In discharging these responsibilities, Admission Forums **should**:

a) refer an objection to the Schools Adjudicator where either it identifies policy, practice or oversubscription criteria of a school that may be unfair, unlawful or that contravene the mandatory provisions of this Code, or where their advice has been disregarded by admission authorities;

b) review the comprehensiveness, effectiveness and accessibility of advice and guidance for parents by the local authority, both through the published composite prospectus (see Appendix 4) and the delivery of Choice Advice (see Appendix 5); and

c) agree, promote and monitor local authority In-Year Fair Access Protocols for potentially vulnerable children including those previously excluded from school, children in care, children with special educational needs and/or disabilities, children who are hard to place, and those who arrive in the area outside the normal admissions round.

Reports on effectiveness of local admission arrangements

4.12 Admission Forums have an important power, under section 85A(1A) of the School Standards and Framework Act 1998 (as inserted by section 41 of the Education and Inspections Act 2006), to publish an annual report. Regulations[67] set out the matters that reports will cover which include:

a) a breakdown of preferences met by ranking (1st, 2nd, 3rd preference etc), and the main factors affecting whether preferences were met;

b) the number of admission appeals made for schools in the area;

c) the ethnic and social mix of pupils attending schools in the area, and factors which affect this;

d) the extent to which existing and proposed admission arrangements serve the interests of vulnerable children;

e) how well In-Year Fair Access Protocols are working and the number of children admitted to each school under the protocol;

f) whether primary schools are complying with infant class size legislation;

g) details of other matters that affect how fairly admission arrangements serve the interests of local children and parents;

h) any recommendation or recommendations that the forum wishes to make in order to improve parental choice and access to education in the local authority's area.

4.13 These reports are a valuable tool in ensuring an open and fair admission system as admission authorities **must** have regard to any advice published by the Admission Forum. The reports will be drawn upon by the Schools Commissioner in drawing up his two yearly national review of fair access.

---

[67] Admission Forum (England) Regulations 2002 (SI 2002/2900) as amended by SI 2007/192

Objections by Parents

4.14 This Code stresses the importance of setting admission arrangements that are clear and easily understood by parents; this is essential if all parents are to feel able to express a preference of school for their child. Individual parents have the right to refer an objection to the Schools Adjudicator if they consider that admission arrangements do not comply with the law or the mandatory requirements of this Code (see paragraph 4.17 below)[68].

Members of Parliament

4.15 Parents may seek support and advice in making an objection from a variety of sources (e.g. local authority admission teams, choice advisers, Citizen Advice Bureaux) but they may also seek the support, advice and assistance of their Member of Parliament. It is for MPs to consider how they can best support their constituents, but they may assist with the completion of a proforma available from the Adjudicator's office for objections. They may also endorse or comment on the objection and provide evidence of the local context, which the Adjudicator may take account of in reaching his determination. Where a group of parents wish to make an objection about the same issue, the MP may facilitate the process of combining these to make the task easier for parents.

The Schools Adjudicator

4.16 The Schools Adjudicator also has a key role in ensuring a fair admissions system by enforcing the requirements of this Code and considering whether any departure from its guidelines has been justified. Once the Adjudicator receives an objection about any maintained school he may consider the admission arrangements for that school as a whole, not just the specific subject of the objection, and the effect of these in the context of all the admission arrangements in the area.

Categories and forms of objections

4.17 The Adjudicator may consider the following categories and forms of objections[69]:

   a) from admission authorities (including local authorities) on any aspect of the admission arrangements for a school for which they are not the admission authority;

---

[68] Section 90(2) of the SSFA 1998

[69] The School Admissions (Alteration and Variation of, and Objections to, Arrangements) (England) Regulations 2007 (SI 2007/496)

b) from Admission Forums on any aspect of the admission arrangements for schools in the area which they cover;

c) from parents who live in the area to pre-existing partially selective admission arrangements, including any partial selection by ability (below the sixth form); any selection by aptitude other than for up to 10% of places in a prescribed or formerly prescribed subject; and any form of pre-existing banding which does not meet the statutory forms of banding provided by section 101 of the School Standards and Framework Act 1998[70];

d) from parents who consider that admission arrangements contain practices or oversubscription criteria that are unlawful or do not comply with the mandatory provisions of this Code;

e) from parents who live in the area to the determination of an admission number which is lower than the one indicated by the net capacity formula[71];

f) from governing bodies of community and voluntary controlled schools to any admission number determined by the local authority for their own school but not to any other aspects of the admission arrangements for their school;

g) from admission authorities (including local authorities) which appeal within seven days against a local authority direction to admit a child in care on the grounds that admission would seriously prejudice the provision of efficient education or the efficient use of resources;

h) from governing bodies of community and voluntary controlled schools to the admission arrangements of other schools within the relevant area, although they may not object to the admission arrangements for other community and voluntary controlled schools whose admission arrangements have been determined by the local authority;

i) from local authorities or governing bodies of any categories of schools to all partially selective admission arrangements. Complaints may be made to the Adjudicator about tests that are not objective, or which appear to test for ability or another aptitude, even where selection for a proportion of places by aptitude is accepted; and

j) from religious authorities about admission arrangements at schools designated as of their faith or denomination.

---

[70] As amended by section 54 of the EIA 2006

[71] The Education (Determination of Admission Arrangements) Regulations 1999 (SI 1999/126) as amended by SI 2002/ 2896 and SI 2007/497

4.18 Adjudicators **must** consider each objection on its individual merits, taking account of the reasons for disagreement at local level and in the light of the legislation and the mandatory provisions and guidelines set out in this Code.

4.19 The Adjudicator's determination is binding. If an admission authority or other party does not implement the determination, the Secretary of State may direct them to do so using his powers under section 497 of the Education Act 1996.

4.20 Objections **should** be made within six weeks of the date on which the objecting body received notification from the admission authority of its determined arrangements, or in the case of objections from parents, within six weeks of the date on which the local authority published a notice in a newspaper stating that admission arrangements had been determined for its area (see paragraph 1.25). Adjudicators have discretion to consider late objections, but will need to be persuaded that it was not reasonably practicable for them to have been submitted earlier.

4.21 Adjudicators are not able to consider objections about aspects of admission arrangements for which other statutory procedures are required. For example, the Adjudicator may consider objections to the admission arrangements of grammar schools, but not about the principle that a grammar school selects its pupils on the basis of high academic ability.

4.22 Adjudicators may uphold, reject or partially uphold objections.

Variation to determined admission arrangements

4.23 Once admission arrangements have been determined for a particular academic year, they cannot be revised except in the very limited circumstances described in paragraphs 4.26 to 4.27 below.

4.24 Regulations (see paragraph 2 of the introduction) permit admission authorities to amend their admission arrangements to ensure that they comply with the law and the mandatory requirements of this Code, for example, to include mandatory criteria, such as those related to children in care, or to remove prohibited criteria or practices, such any of those listed in paragraph 2.13.

4.25 Regulations permit a referral of a proposal to the Schools Adjudicator by an admission authority who considers that as a result of a significant change in circumstance, a variation to admission arrangements is required. There is no statutory definition of a major change of circumstance, but it is considered to be a serious and unexpected event affecting the provision of education at the school.

4.26 Admission authorities **should** consider very carefully whether it is necessary to refer a variation to the Adjudicator. They **must not** do so once parents have been asked to make their decisions, unless a major change in circumstances makes this unavoidable. A request to the Adjudicator for a variation is not always necessary. Changes that would not require a referral include, for example:

a) where a misprint occurred in the published admission arrangements, or where an admission authority has been made aware of the unintended inclusion of unlawful practices in their admission arrangements;

b) where a variation to an admission number is necessary to implement statutory proposals for a prescribed alteration to a school under section 19 of the Education and Inspections Act 2006, irrespective of whether such a variation constitutes a major change. Where such a variation is approved – either by the local authority[72], without modification, or by the Adjudicator – an admission authority is not required to refer the variation to the Adjudicator under section 89(5) of the School Standards and Framework Act 1998. However, where the local authority has modified the admission number, which forms part of the proposals, the variation **must** be referred to the Adjudicator under section 89(5); and

c) where admission arrangements are changed to accommodate a locally agreed in-year fair access protocol for the sharing of children outside the normal admissions round.

---

[72] Following the commencement of Part 2 of the EIA 2006, School Organisation Committees will be abolished and local authorities will assume responsibility for deciding most statutory proposals. References to local authorities in the paragraph should be construed as references to the School Organisation Committee in relation to proposals approved under the provisions of the SSFA 1998 before the commencement of Part 2 of the EIA 2006

4.27 Regulations[73] provide for an admission authority to revise its admission arrangements where it believes this to be necessary to achieve consistency with a decision made in relation to a local school by the Adjudicator, or the Secretary of State, to uphold an objection to another admission authority's admission arrangements. If an admission authority wishes to seek such a revision, it **must** do so within two months of the Adjudicator's decision being made, and **must** notify each of the admission authorities which it was required to consult about the arrangements which it is seeking to revise. Following the amendment of any admission arrangements, the admission authority **must** also notify all the bodies that were consulted before the arrangements were determined about the variation.

---

[73] The School Admissions (Alteration and Variation of, and Objections to, Arrangements) (England) Regulations 2007 (SI 2007/496)

Appendix 1

Other Relevant Legislation

1. This appendix sets out the primary legislation and regulations most relevant to admissions decisions. Admission authorities, adjudicators, appeal panels, local authorities and schools **must** comply with the relevant law as well as acting in accordance with the provisions of this Code and following its guidelines. The information here aims to signpost the relevant law; it does not aim to provide definitive guidance on interpreting the law: that is for the courts.

Sex Discrimination Act 1975

2. Under the Sex Discrimination Act 1975, admission authorities **must not** discriminate between boys and girls in the way they admit them to a school except where the school in question is a single sex school. Admission arrangements for a co-educational school may not be used to achieve a fixed proportion of boys or girls at the school, as this may breach the Act, which requires that at any time an applicant is not disadvantaged on the basis of his or her gender.

Race Relations Acts 1976 and 2000

3. The Race Relations Act 1976 makes it unlawful for admission authorities to discriminate against applicants on the basis of race, colour, nationality or national or ethnic origin. That Act, as amended by the Race Relations (Amendment) Act 2000, imposes on public bodies, including local authorities and schools, a duty to promote racial equality. They **must** have regard to the need to eliminate unlawful racial discrimination; promote equality of opportunity; and promote good relations between people of different racial groups. The governing bodies of schools have specific duties under Articles 3(1), 3(2), 3(3), and 3(5) of the Race Relations Act 1976 (Statutory Duties) Order 2001. Governing bodies **must** have a written statement of their policy for promoting race equality. Local authorities **must** also publish a race equality scheme, which includes similar duties to assess and monitor the effects of their policies, including monitoring admissions to schools. Local authorities are encouraged to use their co-ordinated scheme for allocating school places, for this monitoring purpose.

Human Rights Act 1998

4. The Human Rights Act 1998 confers a right of access to education. This right does not extend to securing a place at a particular school. Admission authorities, however, do need to consider parents' reasons for expressing a preference when they make decisions about the allocation of school places, to take account of the rights of parents under the Act, though this may not necessarily result in the allocation of a place. These might include, for example, the parents' rights to ensure that their child's education conforms to their own religious or philosophical convictions (so far as is compatible with the provision of efficient instruction and the avoidance of unreasonable public expenditure).

Disability Discrimination Acts 1995 and 2005

5. Under the Disability Discrimination Act 1995 admission authorities have a duty not to discriminate against disabled children and prospective pupils in their access to education. Three distinct aspects of admission are specifically covered by the new legislation. Admission authorities **must not** discriminate against a disabled child:

   a) in the arrangements they make for determining pupil admission to the school; or

   b) in the terms on which they offer to admit a disabled child to the school; and

   c) by refusing or deliberately omitting to accept an application for admission.

6. Further guidance on this is given in the Disability Rights Commission Code of Practice.

7. Under the Disability Discrimination Act 2005 public authorities, including schools and local authorities, have a duty when carrying out their functions to have due regard to the need to:

   - promote equality of opportunity for disabled people;

   - eliminate unlawful discrimination;

   - eliminate disability related harassment;

   - promote positive attitudes towards disabled people;

   - encourage disabled people's participation in public life; and

   - take account of disabled people's disabilities even where that involves more favourable treatment.

Local authorities and schools **must** produce and publish a Disability Equality Scheme showing how they will promote equality of opportunity for disabled children, staff and those for whom they provide services, and an annual Action Plan showing how they are carrying out their scheme. The duty applied to secondary schools and local authorities from December 2006 and applies to primary schools and special schools from 3 December 2007.

A Disability Equality Scheme **must** show:

a) how disabled people with an interest in the Scheme have been involved in its development;

b) the methods for assessing the impact of policies and practices on equality for disabled persons;

c) the steps that will be taken to promote equality of opportunity for disabled people;

d) the arrangements for gathering information on the effect of policies and practices on disabled people, including information on recruitment, development and retention of disabled employees; educational opportunities for and achievements of disabled children; and

e) the arrangements for making use of this information to help promote equality of opportunity.

The Disability Equality Scheme covers all the activities of an authority or school and is therefore relevant to admissions.

Equality Act 2006

8.   Section 49 of the Equality Act 2006 sets out provisions in relation to schools. It is unlawful in general for maintained schools, independent schools and non-maintained special schools to discriminate against a person on the grounds of that person's religion or belief in the following ways:

a) in the terms on which it offers to admit him/her as a pupil;

b) by refusing to accept an application to admit him/her as a pupil; or

c) where he/she is a pupil of the establishment:

(i) in the way in which it affords him/her access to any benefit, facility or service;

(ii) by refusing him/her access to a benefit, facility or service;

(iii) by excluding him/her from the establishment; or

(iv)by subjecting him/her to any other detriment.

A "pupil" means any person who receives education at the establishment in question.

9. However, education is a unique area in which to legislate, especially in such areas as discrimination on grounds of religion or belief, both because of the long tradition in this country of schools with a religious character, and because of the requirements on all schools to provide religious education, sex education, and a daily act of worship of a broadly Christian character. Taken alone, the prohibition of discrimination on grounds of religion or belief would create certain difficulties for schools. Certain limited exceptions have therefore been written into the Act to permit important aspects of education in this country to continue to be delivered. Consequently, those schools designated by the Secretary of State as having a religious character (faith schools) are exempt from the provisions making it unlawful to discriminate on the grounds of religion or belief when oversubscribed in the terms on which it offers to admit a child as a pupil or by refusing to accept an application to admit him as a pupil. Other exceptions for faith schools concern:

a) the content of the curriculum; or

b) acts of worship or other religious observance organised by or on behalf of an educational establishment (whether or not forming part of the curriculum).

10. In this context the terms "religion" means any religion and "belief" means any religious or philosophical belief. References to religion or belief do, however, also include a reference to a lack of religion or belief.

11. The body responsible for ensuring that no discrimination takes place differs depending on the type of school. For maintained schools, it will be the local authority or the governing body, depending on who took the decision or action complained of; whereas for independent schools and special schools not maintained by the local authority, the responsible body will be the proprietor of the school.

12. Many schools will already have in place fair, non-discriminatory policies for dealing with pupils and their parents. They may not need to make any change to these in order to comply with the Act. Indeed, schools often lead the way in our multicultural and multi-faith society, in practising and teaching about equality, inclusion and recognising diversity.

13.   However, all schools need to be aware of their obligations and to review their policies and practices to make sure these meet the requirements of the Act, even if they believe that they are already operating in a non-discriminatory way.

14.   The relevant provisions set out that schools (except those designated as having a religious character) will not be allowed to admit or refuse to admit pupils on the basis of religion or belief, or lack of it, and must treat pupils equally irrespective of their or their parents' religion including in relation to providing access to benefits, facilities or services on the same grounds. They also provide that pupils cannot be excluded or subjected to any detriment on the basis of their or their parents' religion or belief (or lack of it).

Admission appeals

15.   Section 94 of the School Standards and Framework Act 1998 provides that parents may appeal against decisions "as to the school at which education is to be provided for the child in the exercise of the authority's functions". Admission authorities are required to inform parents, through the local authority, of their right of appeal, and also to establish panels to which parents can appeal against decisions to refuse admission to preferred schools.

16.   The Education (Admission Appeals) Regulations 2002[74] set out the constitution of admission appeal panels. The School Admission Appeals Code imposes mandatory requirements and provides guidelines on how panels are set up and how hearings are conducted.

17.   Admission authorities **must** admit a child whose parents have won an appeal. If the admission authority wants to challenge the decision of the appeal panel, it may seek judicial review. The Secretary of State has no jurisdiction over the decisions of appeal panels.

---

[74] The Education (Admission Appeals) Regulations 2002 (SI 2002 /2899)

Appendix 2

Admission Forums

1. Admission Forums have a key role in ensuring a fair admissions system that promotes social equity, does not disadvantage one child compared to another and which is straightforward and easy for parents to understand. Forums are responsible for monitoring compliance with this Code and have important powers to publish a report on the effectiveness of local admission arrangements and to refer an objection to the Schools Adjudicator where they consider admission arrangements to be unfair or not in accordance with this Code.

2. The roles and responsibilities of Admission Forums are described in Chapter 4. This appendix provides information and guidelines on Forum membership, tenure, procedures at meetings and how they can promulgate advice. These guidelines should be read in conjunction with the Education (Admission Forums) (England) Regulations 2002, as amended by the Education (Admission Forums) (England) (Amendment) Regulations 2007.

Membership

3. The core membership of Admission Forums is set out in regulations and is shown in the table below:

MEMBERS NOMINATED BY	NUMBER
Local authority – any representative of the authority	1 to 5
Schools – community and voluntary controlled	1 to 3
Schools – foundation	1 to 3
Schools – voluntary aided	1 to 3
Church of England Diocesan Board representatives	1 to 3
Roman Catholic Diocese representatives	1 to 3
Parent Governor representatives	1 to 3
Representatives of the local community	up to 3
Academies	1 per Academy
City Technology Colleges	1 per City Technology College

4. The 2007 regulations require that all maintained schools, except special schools, in the local authority area, nominate a member, if not otherwise represented in the Core membership set out in paragraph 3 above. These are known as 'school members'.

5. The core membership of each forum may ask the local authority to appoint anyone it considers to represent significant interests in the local community, and in accordance with paragraph 3.23 of this Code **must** invite a UK service representative or representatives of other significant concentrations of Crown servants (e.g. GCHQ personnel) to join.

6. Admission Forums **should** include representatives of neighbouring local authorities where, for example, there are significant cross-border issues or they have a contribution to make. These representatives would be in addition to those of the home local authority.

7. Each representative of a school **should** be a head teacher, or a governor (other than one appointed to the school by the local authority who is also a member of the authority).

8. Academies are required by their funding agreements to nominate a representative to be a member of the Admission Forum and to notify the local authority of that nomination. City Technology Colleges are encouraged to take part and to have regard to the advice of the forum. Local authorities **must** invite each CTC in their area to nominate a member.

9. Local authorities **should** appoint representatives from faith groups not already represented, and minority ethnic groups.

10. If the Forum considers that it would be useful to appoint additional members to represent the interests of any section of the local community the local authority **should** appoint such members. For example, where the Forum is considering issues relating to the admission of looked after children, it **should** ask the local authority to appoint local authority officers with expertise in children's social care.

11. Where there is a particular issue that needs investigation and more detailed consideration local authorities **should** create a working group (which does not need to consist of Forum members) to carry out this work and report-back to the Forum.

Tenure

12.	Core members and school members of the forum are appointed for a period not exceeding 4 years, after which they are eligible for reappointment. Other members of the forum are appointed on the terms determined by the core members, including whether or not they are to be eligible for reappointment at the end of their term. Membership of the Forum **should** be reviewed in September each year. If a school, Academy or CTC member ceases to be a head teacher or school governor, they cannot continue on the forum in that capacity.

13.	The local authority may also establish sub-committees to help the Forum in the performance of its functions. Sub-committees might be appropriate for considering primary and secondary issues separately, or, if the relevant area is large and has areas with distinct admissions patterns, separate sub-committees might consider issues in each area, before bringing them back to the main Forum for discussion.

Procedure for meetings and appointment of officers

14.	Regulations require Forums to meet at least twice a year, but the procedure for the meetings is regulated by the core members themselves. All members of the Forum **must** be given at least 7 working days notice of the time and date of the meeting and to be given any documents relevant to that meeting 7 days in advance. While all schools in an area will be members of their Forum, it will not be necessary for them to actively take part in all the work of the Forum and attend all its meetings.

15.	The forum **must** appoint a Chair and Vice Chair, who may or may not be members of the Forum, and a Secretary to convene its meetings.

Promulgating advice and making objections

16.	Admission Forums **should** seek to achieve a consensus among the whole membership rather than secure a majority opinion and **should** only promulgate advice that represents the agreed views of the Forum as a whole. However, where the Forum votes on a proposal to make an objection to the Schools Adjudicator, in order for the objection to be made, the proposal **must** first be approved by a simple majority of all members (not just Core members) voting.

17.	The local authority **must**, as a minimum, publish the Forum's advice on the school admissions section of their website and send copies to all admission authorities in the area. The advice **must** also be included in the composite prospectus published by the local authority each year for parents.

Appendix 3

Statutory Requirement of Co-ordinated Admission Schemes

1. Co-ordinated admission schemes simplify the admission process for parents and establish mechanisms ensuring, so far as reasonably practicable, that every parent of a child living in the local authority area who has applied for a school place in the 'normal admission round' receives an offer of one, and only one, school place on the same day. This appendix sets out the key statutory requirements and obligations placed on local authorities and admission authorities in formulating and establishing schemes.

2. The same regulations now cover secondary schools (defined as schools admitting children at age 11 or later) and primary schools[75] (those schools admitting at ages below 11 which also includes, for this purpose, middle schools[76]).

Agreeing schemes for admission to secondary schools

3. Once local authorities have formulated a scheme for their areas, they **must** pass the scheme for review to the Admission Forum, who may suggest amendments. The local authority **must** then consult all other admission authorities in the area and secure their agreement to the scheme. Academies are required to participate in co-ordinated admission arrangements by their funding agreements. Local authorities **must** seek the views of Academies in their area on the proposed scheme, and their agreement to it, they **must** also invite City Technology Colleges to participate.

Schemes imposed by the Secretary of State

4. If a local authority does not notify the Secretary of State by 15 April that a scheme has been adopted for the following academic year, the Secretary of State may impose a scheme; or where an imposed scheme was in place for the previous year, he may notify the local authority that the scheme will continue for a further year.

---

[75] The School Admissions (Co-ordination of Admission Arrangements) (England) Regulations 2007 (SI 2007/194)

[76] Primary, secondary and middle schools are defined in section 5 of the EA 1996 and further guidance on middle schools is contained in the Education (Middle Schools) (England) Regulations 2002 (SI 2002/1983)

5.   Where the Secretary of State has imposed a scheme and not revoked it a local authority and its schools may decide to adopt the scheme in a subsequent year. If the local authority subsequently adopts a scheme agreed with other admission authorities, in accordance with the regulations, they **must** notify the Secretary of State so that the imposed scheme can be revoked. Where a scheme from a previous year is being adopted, or has been imposed in relation to the previous year (and all admissions authorities have agreed to adopt it for a further year), confirmation **must** be sent to the Secretary of State by 15th April. It will not be necessary to send a copy of the scheme.

6.   Schemes **must** state the mechanism to be used to decide which place will be offered in the event that offers could be made at two or more schools. Schemes **must** stipulate that, wherever possible, parents will receive the highest available preference. If none of the parents' preferences are available the scheme **must** say clearly how a place at another school will be allocated. Another school **must** be allocated unless there are insufficient places remaining in the local authority; in this case, all remaining places **must** be allocated so that a minimum number of children are without the offer of a school place. Schemes **must** also set out how late applications, and arrangements for admissions outside the 'normal admission round' will be handled.

Main obligations imposed by regulations

7.   The main obligations on local authorities and other admission authorities within schemes are:

For secondary schools:

a)   The common application form **must** allow parents to express at least 3 preferences, which may be for schools within or beyond their home local authority area, and the reasons for their preferences.

b)   Local authorities and admission authorities in the area **must** exchange information on applications made and potential offers by the dates specified in the scheme.

c)   Local authorities **must** pass information on applications to other local authorities about applications to schools in their area. The maintaining local authority **must** inform the home local authority if it intends to offer a place, by the dates specified in the scheme.

d) The maintaining local authority **must** tell the home local authority if it could offer a place. The home local authority may take account of this in deciding whether or not to offer the parent a place at a school in its own area, but **must** explain its intentions clearly to parents in its composite prospectus.

e) Offers of places **must** be sent on 1 March (or the next working day if the 1st is not a working day) in the year during which a child will be admitted to school by the home local authority. Schools **must not** contact parents about the outcome of their applications until after these offers have been received. Only the local authority can make an official offer.

f) Parents who cannot be offered one of their preferred schools **must**, if there are places available, be offered a place at another school.

g) While there is no requirement to co-ordinate fully across borders, it is good practice for local authorities to eliminate multiple offers of places across borders and many local authorities already co-ordinate in this way. Regulations provide that where a place can potentially be offered at schools in two or more local authority areas, and the local authorities concerned agree, only one offer of a place is made. Where they do so, schemes **must** specify which local authority will make the offer of a single place. However, it is still possible that some parents who have applied for schools within their own local authority and elsewhere may receive an offer from each local authority.

h) Schemes **must** continue after 1 March to ensure that places which become available are reallocated effectively.

For primary schools:

i) The common application form **must** allow parents to apply for any primary school in their home local authority area, and to give reasons for their preferences. If parents apply direct to a school, the governing body **must** inform the local authority.

j) Parents resident in one local authority who wish to apply for a place at a primary school maintained by another local authority **must** apply through the common application form for the local authority which maintains the school they wish to apply to.

k) Local authorities and admission authorities in the area **must** exchange information on applications made and potential offers by the dates specified in the scheme.

l) Places **must** be offered on the date designated in the scheme by the local authority. Where admission authorities normally admit children to primary school at two or three points in the academic year, they **should** make all offers at the same time. Places allocated to children whose parents have deferred their entry until later in the same academic year cannot be offered to another child, unless the parent withdraws acceptance of the place.

m) A maintaining local authority **must** inform the home local authority if it intends to offer a place at one of its schools to a parent living in a different local authority area. Local authorities **should** exchange information on applications across their borders and seek to eliminate multiple offers across local authority borders wherever possible.

Applications to schools with a different age of transfer

8. The Education (Middle School) (England) Regulations 2002 (SI 2002/1983) define 'Middle Schools' and whether they are classified as primary or secondary schools which depends on the age range of the pupils. For the purposes of co-ordination middle schools with an entry age before 11 are to be treated in the same way as primary schools; upper schools (with an entry age after 11) are to be treated as secondary schools.

9. For middle deemed primary schools, the maintaining local authorities **must** make an application form available and make the offer. For middle deemed secondary schools, the home local authority **must** make an application form available to any parent in the area who wishes to apply to a school in a neighbouring area which operates a different age of transfer. The home local authority **should** accept applications in the same way as it would for its own normal admissions round. It **should**, if preferred schools are in another area, pass forms to neighbouring authorities, who **should** apply their co-ordinated scheme. The maintaining local authority **should** inform the home local authority if a place is to be offered in one of its schools. The maintaining local authority will inform the parent of the outcome of the application.

Appendix 4

Consultation and Publication

1. This appendix provides guidance on consulting on, and the publication of, admission arrangements, and is to be read in conjunction with chapters 1 to 3 of this Code.

Consultation

2. Except in the circumstances described in paragraph 3 below, all admission authorities are required by law to consult by 1 March each year on the admission arrangements for those schools for which they are responsible and, where appropriate, on their proposed co-ordinated admission schemes. Admission authorities **must** consult with their Local Authority, all other admission authorities within the relevant area, the Admissions Forum, admission authorities in neighbouring local authority areas and, in the case of the admission authorities of faith schools, the relevant faith provider group.

3. Individual admission authorities (other than the local authority) can qualify for a one year suspension from the requirement to consult if the local authority has notified the Secretary of State that all admission authorities in the area have consulted each other; that the admission authority is not proposing to change the admission arrangements which it had determined in the preceding year; and that no objection has been made to the Schools Adjudicator about those arrangements in any of the five preceding years. However, governing bodies which qualify for this suspension from the duty to consult **must** still notify statutory consultees of their determination of the school's admission arrangements.

4. Admission arrangements for Academies are approved by the Secretary of State as part of an Academy's funding agreement, which requires it to comply with admissions legislation and the relevant Codes. An Academy **must** consult annually in the same way as other admission authorities do, but cannot alter its admission arrangements without the approval of the Secretary of State. Any objections to an Academy's admission arrangements will be considered by the Secretary of State.

5. Admission authorities **must** consult on the full details of admission arrangements they propose to determine, which **must** be consistent with the co-ordinated scheme operating in the area in the year in question, and **should** include:

a) admission numbers for any years to which it is intended to admit pupils, including Year 12;

b) application procedures;

c) the oversubscription criteria to be used in accordance with the provisions of chapters 1 and 2 of this Code, and the order in which they will be applied, to allocate places if the school receives more applications than there are places available;

d) information about any tests for aptitude or ability if allowed;

e) any separate entry requirements and oversubscription criteria for Year 12 or nursery places, if applicable;

f) information about whether a waiting list will be maintained and for how long after 1 September;

g) information about how late applications can be made and how they will be handled, as agreed in the co-ordinated scheme.

Informing parents: publication of admission arrangements

6.   Parents need to be able to make informed decisions when applying for a school place for their children. They **should** have all relevant information to hand before they apply. It is easier for parents to understand local admissions systems that are clear, fair and objective. Above all, they need to be able to understand whether they have a realistic chance of being offered a place for their child at any particular school.

7.   Local authorities **must** publish, in hard copy, a composite prospectus annually with information about admission arrangements in their area (Education (School Information) (England) Regulations 2002). There is much existing good practice for admission authorities to draw on when bringing together and publishing information. Parents find it helpful to have information on all primary schools in their area in one booklet; similarly it is helpful for the information on secondary schools, including Academies, Trust Schools and CTCs, to be in one book. Local authorities **must** also publish this information fully on their website and enable parents to make online applications. Admission Forums **should** consider the information made available to parents and advise local authorities on what more is needed to raise the standard to that of the best.

8.   Published admissions information:

a) **should** offer clear guidance in plain English and in commonly used community languages to steer parents through the procedure;

b) **must** set out clearly the timescale for each stage of the admissions process, in particular the deadline for the receipt of applications (including on-line applications) (Education (School Information) (England) Regulations 2002) and **must** include the date on which parents will be sent the outcome as agreed in the co-ordinated scheme (locally agreed date for primary; 1 March for secondary).

c) **must** explain the admission arrangements of all maintained schools and Academies in the area, including how co-ordinated schemes work in the local authority's area and neighbouring areas (where appropriate). Published admission arrangements **must** include the oversubscription criteria that will be used to allocate places if there are more applicants than places at a particular school in accordance with the provisions of Chapters 1 and 2 of this Code;

d) **should** explain what tests will be used and when (where appropriate);

e) **must** give information on the number of applications for places at each school the previous year, the number which were successful (Education (School Information) (England) Regulations 2002) and **should** give the criteria under which they were accepted (with an indication of whether this reflects the pattern of recent years). Parents **should** be made aware that they need to consider whether they meet the oversubscription criteria carefully;

f) **should** explain what is expected from parents, and what the parent can expect from the school and the local authority, at each stage;

g) **must** make clear how parents can express their preferences for a school, when parents will know whether or not their applications have been successful, and how to take up their statutory right of appeal (Education (School Information) (England) Regulations 2002);

h) **should** include explanations to help parents assess realistically their likelihood of getting a place at any preferred school;

i) **should** set out the details of the agreed fair access protocol for the sharing of children outside the normal admissions round with an explanation that children without a school place **must** take precedence over children on a waiting list attending another school;

j) **must** give a name and details of a contact point for further information (Education (School Information) (England) Regulations 2002).

9.   In addition to the published information, it is good practice for local authorities to work with schools and other partners to offer targeted Choice Advice to parents who are unable or unsure about how to use the information on school admissions. Choice Advice may be delivered in or out of school and **should** take the form of group or one-to-one sessions for those needing additional support. The aim of these sessions is to ensure that every parent has the right information to make the optimum choice possible for their child. Detail of how Choice Advice might operate is contained in Appendix 5.

Appendix 5

Choice Advice – Guidelines for Local Authorities

Introduction

1. All children of all backgrounds, race or religion, must have the same degree of access to good quality schools. Children must not be disadvantaged because their parents have difficulty in accessing the information they need to make a choice of school or because their parents do not, for whatever reason, engage with the process of applying for a school. In order for all children to have the best chance in life, it is essential that their parents and carers have the information they need to make decisions about which schools to apply for and, where they need it, support in making the application.

2. The transition between primary and secondary school can be one of the most difficult times for families and children. Most parents and carers recognise the critical importance of getting a place in a secondary school that will meet their children's academic and developmental needs, is easy to travel to, and where their children will be happy and want to attend.

3. Admission arrangements can often appear complex and this Code makes clear the importance of ensuring straightforward procedures that are easily understood and that all families can access and navigate. Whilst the majority of families, armed with information about the schools in their area, are able to navigate the system successfully and gain a school place that meets their requirements, there are a number of families who will still find the system difficult to understand and challenging to operate. There are also a small number of parents who, for one reason or another, are unable or unwilling to engage with the process. This tends to happen more frequently in the most deprived communities and puts the children affected at a significant disadvantage.

4. In order to ensure that these children are able to attend a school that will meet their needs and have the opportunity to realise their full potential as all children should, the Government has provided funding for local authorities to establish an independent Choice Advice service in their area. Choice Advice will enable those parents who find it hardest to engage with, and navigate, the admissions system to make informed decisions about which schools will best meet their child's needs.

Statutory duty to provide support for parents

5. Section 42 of the Education and Inspections Act 2006 amends section 81 of the School Standards and Framework Act 1998 to place a duty on local authorities to provide advice and assistance to all parents with children of school age in their area, when they are deciding which schools they want to send their children to. Choice Advice is one way that local authorities can discharge this duty for more disadvantaged parents at the secondary school transfer stage.

Choice Advisers

6. The primary aim of Choice Advisers is to empower those parents who may struggle with the admissions system, to make informed and realistic choices of which secondary school to apply for in the best interest of their child. Choice Advisers do not take decisions for parents and cannot guarantee a place at a particular school, but the service will place these families on a level playing field with all other families when making the important decision of which secondary schools to apply for.

7. The role of Choice Advisers is to help families optimise their choices using all the information to hand as detailed below, and use local knowledge of what individual schools have to offer to ensure parents are more likely to get the best place for their child. Where appropriate, this will include information about schools which might be in different local authority areas with additional advice covering local authority school admission regimes and individual schools' admission criteria.

8. Choice Advisers are expected to know about:

    a) How the **co-ordinated admissions** system works in their own, and neighbouring, local authority areas when schools in that area might be available to the child to attend.

    b) **Admission policies** for the appropriate community, voluntary aided, foundation, Trust, independent and boarding schools and Academies which might be available to the child to attend.

    c) **Performance and value-added data** for appropriate schools.

    d) **The Ofsted report** of the last inspection of the school.

    e) **Admissions data** from previous years including the number of applications received, number of children admitted and success rate of appeals.

    f) The **school's own description** of their offer contained in their prospectus and their online School Profile, including their ethos and any special facilities.

g) **Special needs and disability policy and provision**, drawing on the knowledge and experience of local parent-partnership services.

h) Details of the curriculum offer including the **school's specialism** in the case of Specialist Schools.

i) **Times of the school day** and **term dates** including any knowledge of proposals to change the pattern of education provision.

j) **Transport details** including financial assistance to help with the cost of travel to and from school and home–school distances.

k) Details of **school uniform policy** and how families can obtain financial assistance to help with the cost.

l) **E-admissions** and online applications.

9. Local authorities **should** make Choice Advice available to families living within their boundary irrespective of where their children attend primary school. Where a family requiring support is identified at a primary school in one local authority area and they reside in another, local authorities **should** work together to ensure that the family receives Choice Advice from the most appropriate source. This is very likely to arise in large conurbations covered by a number of authorities.

10. It is widely recognised that those working in local authority admissions teams have an important role to play in advising parents about school places and for most families, this, coupled with the information available about school places and the process, is sufficient enough to enable them to confidently choose which schools to express a preference for. Some families, often the most disadvantaged, require extra support and want this to be from a professional. Every local authority **should** provide Choice Advice for families in their area who need it. Local authorities have the flexibility in deciding how best to deliver their Choice Advice service locally, but **must** provide an independent service that is focused on the needs of children in the transition between primary and secondary school whose families would normally find this process difficult to negotiate.

11.   The independence of the service gives assurances that there is no conflict between the need of the local authority to allocate places at its schools and the advice parents receive. Local authorities can secure the independence of the service in a variety of ways for example, by contracting it out to the voluntary sector or incorporating it into the Children's Information or Parent Partnership Services. Where local authorities deliver the service through drawing together existing transition programmes or through their admissions team, in order to avoid any conflict of interests for the individuals, they **must** ensure as a minimum, that the Choice Advisers are not in the same management chain or reporting lines as the local authority's admissions staff. They must also satisfy themselves that the advice on offer is genuinely independent and includes impartial advice on <u>all</u> relevant local schools, including those not within the local authority's own area as appropriate. Whatever model local authorities choose, they **must** ensure that the Choice Advisers work closely with the admissions staff and schools to ensure the effective sharing of information, so that parents are offered the most appropriate advice and support they need.

12.   These guidelines are intended to help local authorities develop their own approach to Choice Advice in a way that best suits their local needs. Further guidance on establishing an independent Choice Advice service, example delivery models, information on training and accreditation, and an outline person-specification and job-description are available on the Choice Advice website at www.dfes.gov.uk/choiceadvice. This also includes case studies of good practice taking place around England.

Targeting Choice Advice

13.   Nationally, research shows that around 6% of parents with children transferring to secondary school are not interested in choosing a school. This often means that there is a small group of children who do not have a secondary school place when they leave primary school and some are allocated a place that is not suitable. Traditionally these children are at the greatest risk of slipping through the net and disappearing from the system. These are the families that Choice Advisers will target and focus their advice on and they **should**, where appropriate, offer one-to-one support.

14.   The Choice Advice service **should** also support disadvantaged families in maximising the likelihood of their successfully securing a place in the school that will best meet their children's needs.

15.   The service **should** be made available to all members of the family who have responsibility for the child and want extra support, including fathers and mothers and those who are not normally resident with the child, as well as any adults with caring responsibility. Wherever possible, the child **should** be included in any discussions and provided with appropriate advice so that they are able to express an informed view about their future school place.

Quality Assurance

16.   Parents must have confidence in the advice they receive and will need to know that it is unaffected by any potential political or administrative considerations at play in the local authority or local schools.

17.   There are measures in place to secure the independence of the Choice Advisers, in particular through:

    a. a clear status as an independent professional, accredited through the Support and Quality Assurance network;

    b. an online forum at www.dfes.gov.uk/choiceadvice, where Choice Advisers can access support and advice about issues and share best practice; and

    c. evaluation of the impact of the service, including analysis of parental satisfaction data.

Appendix 6

Guidelines for boarding schools

1. This appendix provides guidelines for the admission authorities for maintained boarding schools on assessing suitability for boarding. All of the mandatory requirements and guidelines of this Code apply to schools with boarding places unless an explicit exception is made. This appendix only applies to boarding places.

Suitability for boarding

2. It is the responsibility of the admission authority to ensure that processes to ascertain suitability for boarding are carried out in line within the local co-ordination schemes timetable for the exchange of information. The Admission authority **should** give adequate notice of the deadline by which any information will be required, but **must not** determine that a candidate is unsuitable to board simply because information cannot be made available by that deadline. Admission authorities **must** make reasonable efforts to obtain this information before the published deadline for receipt and final consideration of applications.

3. In accordance with paragraph 2.13(o) of this Code the assessment of suitability for boarding **must** be separate from a school's oversubscription criteria and **must** be undertaken prior to the school applying its oversubscription criteria.

Assessing suitability for boarding

4. Section 88A of the School Standards and Framework Act 1998 (inserted by section 44 of the Education and Inspections Act 2006) prohibits the use of interviews to determine admission to a maintained school, except where an interview is used solely to assess the suitability of an applicant for a boarding place.

5. When assessing suitability for boarding, admission authorities **must** only consider the following two conditions:

   a) Whether a child presents a serious health and safety hazard to other boarders; or

   b) Whether a child is developmentally suited to a boarding place.

6. The admission authorities for maintained boarding schools may also use supplementary information forms in order to assess suitability for boarding in accordance with paragraph 1.74 and to the extent that it is necessary to determine boarding need in accordance with paragraph 2.55 of this Code.

7. Sample supplementary information forms are available at www.dfes.gov.uk/sacode Admission authorities may use their own forms providing that in doing so they comply with the mandatory requirements and guidelines of this Code.

8. In order to determine the suitability of an applicant to board, an admission authority may therefore have regard to:

    a) The outcome of an interview with the applicant carried out for that sole purpose;

    b) Information provided by the applicant's current school or – if he or she is currently out of school – previous school, requested and provided for the same purpose;

    c) Information provided by the home local authority on safeguarding issues.

9. Admission authorities **must not** use any other process to determine suitability for boarding.

10. Where there are more applicants who are suitable to board than there are boarding places available, the admission authority **must** apply the oversubscription criteria set out in its published admission arrangements. These criteria **must** be set in accordance with the provisions of this Code and legal requirements (such as, for instance, giving top priority to children in care) and **must not** amount to any form of selection by aptitude or ability, except where otherwise permitted. In accordance with paragraph 2.13(o) boarding schools **must not** give priority to children on the grounds that they are more suitable than other applicants when they have more applicants, who are assessed as suitable for boarding, than boarding places available.

General principles

11. For boarding places, admission authorities for mainstream schools are entitled to take the view that a history of major behavioural difficulties such as sexual misconduct, arson or extreme physical violence is likely to render an applicant unsuitable to board. Low level misbehaviour would not do so.

12. Schools **must not** ask for or consider information on religious background (unless this is relevant to assessment against published admission arrangements), home circumstances, academic ability, sporting or artistic ability, academic interests or other extraneous matters such as low level misbehaviour. If any such information is provided it **must** be disregarded.

13. If an admission authority determines that an applicant is not suitable for boarding, it **must** inform the parents/carers in writing of the reasons for the determination and, as with other refusals of admission (i.e. for a day place), the right of appeal and who to contact to lodge an appeal.

Health and safety risk to other children

14. Unless children have been permanently excluded from a maintained school two or more times, admission authorities **must not** refuse to admit children who have a history of serious misbehaviour if they have been assessed by the local authority as suitable for a mainstream school place. However, it is recognised that a boarding place for such children, in a mainstream environment, is unlikely to be appropriate if a child has a serious proven record (i.e. not based on unsubstantiated accusations) of sexual misconduct, arson, or physical violence.

Developmental suitability for a boarding place

15. Where using interviews to determine suitability, boarding schools **must**:

    a) focus purely on whether the applicant would be able to cope with and benefit from a boarding environment;

    b) be fair and open. Children and parents **must** be informed of the process in advance, and know what to expect from the interview; and

    c) give children a chance to state separately from their parents or guardians whether they wish to board.

Interviews to establish suitability for boarding

16. An admission authority may only interview an applicant as part of a process to determine whether or not he/she is suitable to board. Admission authorities which use interviews **must** focus purely on whether the applicant would be able to cope with and benefit from a boarding environment.

17. Questions **must** be restricted to the following areas, although schools are free to develop their own sets of questions within these areas. An inadequate response in any particular area would not necessarily mean that a child was not suitable overall to board:

a) Experience of staying away from his/her parents/carers or reliance staying away from home.

b) Experience of sharing a room with other children/communal living and whether the applicant shows an understanding that in a boarding environment he/she would be expected to take into account the needs of others and to compromise.

c) Has the applicant thought about the implications of boarding (e.g. what he/she would like most about boarding school and what he/she would miss most about home)?

d) Whether a boarding place is what the child wants and is not just the wishes of a parent/carer.

e) Is there any medical reason why boarding would not be appropriate which could not be met by reasonable adjustment to the boarding accommodation, routine and practice within the school's responsibilities under the Disability Discrimination Act and other responsibilities?

Information from Schools

18.   Admission authorities **must not** use references from schools as any part of an admissions process other than to assist in the determination of an applicant's suitability for boarding.

Information from Local Authorities

19.   On receipt of an application (or enquiry), an admission authority may also seek information from the child's home local authority to ascertain whether an applicant may present a safeguarding risk such that their admission would put him/herself or other children at serious risk.

Glossary

Admission Authority

The body responsible for setting and applying a school's admission arrangements. For community or voluntary controlled schools, the Local Authority is the admission authority; and for foundation or voluntary aided schools, the governing body of the school is the admission authority. For Academies the funding agreement states who is responsible for applying admissions arrangements (in most cases the Academy itself) but Academies can only set or alter their admission arrangements with the prior agreement of the Secretary of State.

Admission Arrangements

The overall procedure, practices and oversubscription criteria used in deciding the allocation of school places.

Admissions Criteria (see also 'oversubscription criteria')

The list of criteria an admission authority must adopt for its school(s) which are used only when the school is oversubscribed to assess which children will be offered a place. Once determined, admissions criteria, including the admission number, must be published by the school and in the local authority composite prospectus at least 6 weeks before parents express their preferences.

Admission Forum

A statutory local body charged with co-ordinating the effectiveness and equity of local admission arrangements with a statutory right of objection to these. Consists of representatives of admission authorities, dioceses, the local community, parent governors and academies.

Admission Number (or Published Admission Number)

The number of school places that the admission authority must offer in each relevant age group of a school for which it is admission authority. Admission numbers are part of a school's admission arrangements, and must be consulted upon with the rest of a school's admission arrangements and be published with those arrangements in the school's prospectus and the local authority composite prospectus. .

Banding

A system of oversubscription criteria in which all children applying for a place at a banding school are placed into ability bands based on their performance in a test or other assessment. Places are then allocated so that the school's intake either reflects the ability profile of those children applying to the school, those children applying to a group of schools banding jointly, the local authority ability profile or the national ability profile.

Catchment area

A geographical area, from which children may be afforded priority for admission to a school. A catchment area is part of a school's admission arrangements and must therefore be consulted upon, determined and published in the same way as other admission arrangements.

Children in Public Care; Looked After Children; Children in Care

Children who are in the care of local authorities as defined by section 22 of the Children Act 1989. In relation to school admissions legislation a 'looked after child' is only considered as such if the local authority confirms he or she will be in public care when he or she is admitted to a school.

Choice Advice

An independent service commissioned by local authorities to support families who need the most help during the admissions round to make the best and most realistic choice of secondary school for their children. Choice advisers assist parents through the decision making process but must not take the decision for them.

Common Application Form

The form parents complete and submit to local authorities listing their preferred choices of schools when applying for a school place for their child as part of the local co-ordination scheme during the normal admissions round. Parents must be allowed to express a preference for a minimum of 3 secondary or 1 primary school on the relevant common application form as determined by their local authority. Local authorities may afford parents a higher number of preferences if they wish.

Composite prospectus

The prospectus that a local authority is required to publish at least six weeks before parents express their preferences for schools. This prospectus must include detailed admission arrangements of all maintained schools in the area (including admission numbers and catchment areas).

Conditionality

Oversubscription criterion that stipulates conditions that affect the priority given to an application, for example taking account of other preferences or giving priority to families who include in their other preferences a particular type of schools (e.g. where other schools are of the same religious denomination). Conditionality is prohibited by this Code.

Co-ordination/Co-ordinated scheme

Co-ordinated schemes must be consulted upon across all relevant admission authorities and determined in the year prior to which they are to apply. All local authorities are required to co-ordinate primary and secondary admissions for all schools in their area. Although individual admission authorities rank all applicants in order of priority for admission, offers are sent out by the local authority on 1 March for secondary pupils and on an agreed date for primary pupils.

First Preference First

Oversubscription criterion that giving priority to children according to the order of other schools named as a preference by their parents, or only considering applications stated as a first preference. The First Preference First oversubscription criterion is prohibited by this Code.

Governing Bodies

School governing bodies are bodies corporate responsible for conducting schools with a view to promoting high standards of educational achievement. Governing bodies have three key roles: setting strategic direction, ensuring accountability and monitoring and evaluation.

Grammar Schools (designated)

These are the 164 schools designated under section 104(5) of the School Standards and Framework Act 1998 as grammar schools. A 'grammar school' is defined by section 104(2) of the Act as a school which selects all (or substantially all) of its pupils on the basis of general (i.e. academic) ability.

Home-School Agreements

A statement explaining: the school's aims and values; the school's responsibilities towards its pupils who are of compulsory school age; the responsibilities of the pupil's parents; and what the school expects of its pupils.

Infant Class Size Exceptions

These are prescribed exceptions to the statutory requirement that infant classes must be no more than 30 per school teacher. These are: the admission of looked after children outside the normal admission round; the admission of pupils for whom no other maintained school is available within the area; children admitted on appeal; a child who was originally refused a place in error; and statemented pupils whose statements name the school. In all these cases the class can only remain oversize for the school year and qualifying measures must be taken to ensure that the class size regulations are complied with for following years.

Infant Class Size Limit

The School Standards and Framework Act 1998 requires children aged 5, 6, and 7 to be taught in classes of no more than 30 per school teacher.

Local Government Ombudsman

An independent, impartial and free service that investigates complaints about maladministration of certain public bodies.

Local Offer Date

The date set by local authorities, in agreement with local primary schools, on which offers for primary school places are sent out throughout the year (i.e. may be termly).

Looked After Children (see Children in Public Care above)

National offer date

The date on which local authorities are required to send the offer of a school place to all parents of secondary age pupils in their area. The national offer date is the 1 March each year, or next working day. For primary schools, see 'Local offer date'.

Net Capacity

The capacity of a school is the number of pupil places available. The net capacity is intended to provide a single, robust and consistent method of assessing the capacity of schools. For further guidance, see www.dfes.gov.uk/netcapacity.

Oversubscription

Where a school has a higher number of applicants than the school's published admission number each year.

Oversubscription criteria (see also 'admissions criteria')

This refers to the published criteria that an admission authority applies when a school has more applications than places available in order to decide which children will be allocated a place.

Qualifying Measures

The actions taken by an admission authority to ensure that the statutory obligation that requires infant classes of 5, 6, and 7 year olds to contain no more than 30 pupils per school teacher, such as the reorganisation of the class or employment of another teacher must be taken to bring the class within the class size limit for the next academic year.

Reception Class

Defined by section 142 of the School Standards and Framework Act 1998. An entry class to primary schools for children who are aged 5 during the school year and for children who are younger than 5 who it is expedient to educate with them.

Relevant Age Group

The age group to which children are normally admitted. Each relevant age group must have admission arrangements, including an admission number attached. Some schools (for example schools with sixth forms which admit children into the sixth form) have more than one relevant age group.

Relevant Area

The area for a school (determined by its local authority and then reviewed every two years) within which the admission authority for that school must consult all other prescribed schools on its admission arrangements.

Rising Fives

The term rising fives usually relates to children who are still age four at the start of a school year but will reach age 5 before the year is over.

Schools Adjudicator

A statutory officer who is appointed by the Secretary of State for Education and Skills but is independent of him. The Adjudicator decides on objections to published admission arrangements and variations of determined admission arrangements. The Schools Adjudicator comes under the supervision of the Council on Tribunals.

Statement of Special Educational Need (SEN)

A legal document issued by the local authority specifying the particular needs, resources and provision required to support the child, and can include a named school that is suitable for providing education for that child.

Twice Excluded Pupils

A child who has been permanently excluded from two or more maintained schools.

Waiting Lists

A list of children held and maintained by the admission authority when the school has allocated all its places, on which children are ranked in priority order against the school's published oversubscription criteria. There is no statutory requirement for admission authorities to set up and maintain waiting lists but where they do places must be allocated in accordance with the school's published admission arrangements.

Index

References are to paragraph locators, not page numbers.
G = Glossary